Positive Thinking in a Dark Age

ESSAY~
GLOBAL 1

Jim Tull

Puma Negra Publishing
New Orleans, Louisiana

Jim Tull
87 Reservoir Road
Chepachet, RI 02814
jtull@ccri.edu

Ordering Information:
To order print copies, contact the author at the address above.
Discounts are available on quantity purchases.

All author proceeds from the sale of this book (print and electronic versions) will be donated to La Via Campesina, a global movement supporting small and medium-size farmers, landless people, women farmers, indigenous people, migrants and agricultural workers. Visit their website for more information: www.viacampesina.org

Positive Thinking in a Dark Age/ Jim Tull. —1st ed.
Puma Negra Publishing — www.csdrury.com/pumanegrapublishing

Library of Congress Control Number 2016952651
ISBN 978-0-9914409-2-4 (Paperback)

Cover Design: Max Reinhardsen
Photo Credit: Laura Sage

Dedicated to Australopithecus afarensis

Contents

Introduction vii

Block Power 1

Titanistad Abandon...7

What We Think Is What We Get 13

Deep Bullshit.. 23

One Less Car on the Road 31

I Had a Martin Luther King Dream 41

Shall the Poor Always Be with Us? 51

Out of Love 61

Saint Dorothy.. 71

School Reform: A Systems View.......................... 77

Secret Lessons of Francis of Assisi 83

Memoirs of the Oldest (and Guiltiest) Man...................... 91

What Does It Mean to Give Up on Our World? 107

How I Backed into Loving the World............................ 115

Gratitude... 129

Introduction

A progressive activist fresh out of college, I took my first job, a teaching position, under Stan Ward, conservative and much older. "The world's gonna look pretty much like it does now in forty years," he insisted. "Nothing's gonna change."

It was 1976 and the faculty was assigned to read Robert F. Bundy's essay "Social Visions and Educational Futures," asking educators if they were preparing students for a 'post-industrial' future (= dramatically changed) or a 'super-industrial' one (= status quo, embellished). I embraced the challenge of the essay. Stan knew what future world I was aiming for (big change), and he also knew I had little faith in the viability of the current trajectory. Pick the poison in it — mass starvation, nuclear oblivion, environmental ruin, stagflation. Just the same, he replied, "It'll be much like it is today, with a few more gadgets."

Forty years later has arrived, and I hear Stan's avuncular chuckle. Smart phone screens have replaced cathode ray tubes (TV), but either way people are still just staring at screens. The air's still too filthy to breathe comfortably — in Shanghai now more than LA. War clearly remains with us, though it's a bit different. Nuclear winter never arrived. Life today is just a more and bigger and quicker and flatter and more complicated and stressful version of life forty years past. "Pretty much the same," in other words, as predicted by my elder.

If Stan were still here, I would defend my side by pointing out that nuclear winter never arrived because I *prevented* it from arriving (You're welcome, Stanchildren!). I would also throw him this one from MIT economist, Rudi Bornbusch: "In economics [and...], things take longer to happen than you think they will, and then they happen faster than you thought they could."

The collapse of a civilization — or of civilization, as a form of social organization, itself — is more likely anyhow to *appear* as a slow, perhaps even imperceptible, descent rather than a sudden implosion. An unraveling, not so much a collapse, as we might imagine, punctuated nevertheless by sudden drops, like ice migrating from Greenland into the North Atlantic. A long, slow trickle with occasional, massive glacier slides.

Probably the biggest change typifies the imperceptibly slow — the dominant culture, now global in reach, is disintegrating even as it continues to spread, due to young people at its center increasingly losing faith in its values and program. Glued to their candy bar-size chunks of screen-coated plastic, they nevertheless recognize the emptiness of their entertainment and relationships. And their lives. To support this observation I am not in need of academic surveys. Each year, nearly two hundred college students sit around in my classroom circles and echo the same refrain: "This sucks." Twenty years ago there was a more lively debate and discussion. Not now. Not much more five years ago. The conversation these days moves directly to, "what do we do about 'this'?" An eerily sober moment of truth exposed.

The students are among the relatively privileged young people for whom the global systems have been designed to *benefit*. The *winners* of the global zero-sum game of Life™. Pathetically, the winners are toggling somewhere between chronic, low-level anxiety and acute misery. The dying culture's defense mechanism is to normalize the pain, lower the bar, locate the pain in the individual, normalize more, medicalize and drug, offer happy-making stuff to buy, normalize.

Over the past forty years, the years since Stan and my first job out of college, the progressive in me has slipped into something more radical (= searching for the 'root', yes). I see the change Stan could not, and I anticipate more rapid and profound change, at the very least, coming ahead. The decline of one world, too, and the ascendance of *some*thing else. Call it a 'post-industrial' society, or societ*ies*, or use another label.

The essays collected in this volume, written over the past fifteen years (please excuse redundancies!), reflect neither optimism nor hope for humanity's future. Thinking positively and making an active commitment to create a just and sustainable future requires neither of these. Likewise, making and/or relying on predictions serves very narrow and limited purposes. How the 21st century turns out, for instance, is anyone's guess and no one's certainty. One outcome of the century might be an improved quality of human life and a richer and healthier biosphere. Positive thinking applied to an active commitment to nurture change means, for me, aiming for a possibility of this sort. It is my belief, most certainly reflecting my values, observation and study, that the quality of human life on the planet, though it most certainly can worsen, is currently very poor, on balance. The glitter and shininess of parts of our experience reflect, at best, relatively shallow and ephemeral pleasure. They also reflect, and mask, a deep and often hidden dis-ease. Then on another level, more people, in absolute numbers, are enduring chronic destitution than at any other time in history. Human discontent and population growth, serviced by our extractive global economy, are at the same time draining the life out of the planet, as fertile and vibrant and diverse and resilient as our home (still) is and appears so beautifully in many places to be.

My intention in writing is to provide tools for transition, tools that pry open possible futures. Through these essays I continue to merge into the growing corps of midwives scattered and also networked, welcoming with encouragement what Joanna Macy is calling the 'Great Turning'.

Our transition may be for the better, Stan, or it may be for the worse. But it's going to be different. Very different.

"We live fragmented, compartmentalized lives in which contradictions are carefully sealed off from each other...We do this not through conscious design or because we are not intelligent or capable, but because of the way in which deep cultural undercurrents structure life in subtle but highly consistent ways that are not consciously formulated."

— Edward T. Hall

"We were taught to believe that the will to dominate and conquer folks who are different from ourselves is natural, not culturally specific...There are paradigms for the building of human community that do not privilege domination."

— bell hooks

"The major problems in the world are the result of the differences between the way nature works and the way people think."

— Gregory Bateson

"For the Indigenous Souls of all people who can still remember how to *be* real cultures, life is a race to be elegantly run, not a race to be competitively won. In cannot be won; it is the gift of the world's diverse beautiful motion that must be maintained."

— Martín Prechtel

"What if we discover that our present way of life is irreconcilable with our vocation to become fully human?"

— Paulo Freire

"An economy genuinely local and neighborly offers to localities a measure of security that they cannot derive from a national or a global economy controlled by people who, by principle, have no local commitment."

— Wendell Berry

"In nature's economy the currency is not money, it is life."

— Vandana Shiva

"Rats in the laboratory, when threatened, are observed to busy themselves in frenzied, irrelevant activities. So apparently do we...It helps to change the norms from individual, competitive self-interest to collective, systemic self-interest."

— Joanna Macy

"The people of the Middle Ages didn't think of themselves as being in the 'middle' of anything at all. No paradigm is ever able to imagine the next one. It's almost impossible for one paradigm to imagine that there will even *be* a next one...If the world is saved, it will not be by old minds with new programs but by new minds with no programs at all."

— Daniel Quinn

"Hunger, poverty, environmental degradation, economic instability, unemployment, chronic disease, drug addiction, and war persist in spite of the analytical ability and technical brilliance that have been directed toward eradicating them...They will yield only as we reclaim our intuition, stop casting blame, see the system as the source of its own problems, and find the courage and wisdom to *restructure* it."

— Donella Meadows

"If we wait for the governments, it'll be too little, too late
If we act as individuals, it'll be too little
But if we act as communities, it might just be enough, just in time."

— transitionus.org

"There is no power for change greater than a community discovering what it cares about. "

— Margaret Wheatley

Block Power[*]

"People know what they do.

And most know why they do what they do.

But what they don't know is what what they do does."

— Michael Foucault

Nobody went to jail. No one burned down the State House or forcibly removed the President of the United States from office. What a few people on our city block on the south side of Providence decided to do instead was something more radical, if less dramatic. We tried to get our neighbors to turn to each other a little bit more for personal support.

The Project

Before purchasing a two-family house on Gallatin Street, my family lived just two streets away in a three-family limited-equity cooperative, which we had converted from a private residence owned by an absentee landlord. Like most city folks, we knew our immediate neighbors enough to greet them by

[*] Original publication: "Block Power," *Dark Mountain*, September 2014.

name. The other block residents were mostly nameless faces. But when we purchased our new home I resolved to greet each new neighbor I bumped into, learn names and addresses and introduce myself. I met a lot of people and recorded each name on a map I created of the thirty-six-household block. But early on I discovered that my new neighbors seemed to know each other a fair bit more than neighbors did on my old block. I learned that eight years prior to our move a college student living on the block chose to organize a block party to fulfill a requirement for a class he was taking. The party became an annual event and naturally created a greater sense of community.

A few years after our move, as I was getting to know more neighbors, and coincidentally rethinking my assumptions about social change, I became convinced that building community — local, very small scale networks — was a more radical path to social transformation and ecological sustainability than what I was doing in my vocational life. For work, I was feeding the hungry, sheltering the homeless, witnessing in direct action for peace and justice and trying, through coalition work, to get the government (and other institutions) to meet human needs and respect human rights. All the while I was living simply and riding my bike everywhere. These activities I was so devoted to (and still am to a degree) were important and useful, but not radical, not directly to the point of solving social problems much less of saving humanity or creating a better way to live.

Starting where I lived, I decided to take an active role in our informal, unincorporated, unnamed block association and encourage my neighbors to step beyond the more usual block activity and try to create a 'consultation exchange' directory. This tool would obligate residents, upon request, to provide initial consultation to a neighbor about something they are skilled at or know about. We reasoned that neighbors would enjoy sharing what they know in this way, but not be so inclined to actually do the work itself (to care for an elderly parent or replace a roof). It's a first step to get neighbors to do for each other what many of us do for our friends and family — offer advice before seeking professional service. Of course, the initial help is sometimes sufficient and we are spared the need to spend.

Of the thirty-six households on our block (demographically, about eighty percent African-American, ten percent Latino and ten percent white, including working class, middle class professionals and families surviving on public assistance), thirty-three participated in creating the directory. Carolyn, the mom of the former college student who organized the first block party, needed herself to complete a service project toward a college degree and conducted most of the interviews. She simply asked, "What do you know about? What do you know how to do that you might share in some way to help out a neighbor?" Many residents were slow to identify a skill or something they know that could be of use to a neighbor. They could make a list of needs they have or problems in the neighborhood, but they needed some prodding to name something they know about worthy of sharing. We needed to convince some that their skill/knowledge might potentially come in handy. I went ahead and listed 'philosophy' as something I know about, anticipating that one of our neighbors might just return from her first semester in college and declare to her parents that she wanted to major in the subject. Then I get the call and the troubleshooting begins. Unlikely, but you never know.

Project Significance

We compiled a list and directory, with names, addresses and phone numbers and what each know or could do. The range of 'gifts' hidden in our houses — 'unwrapped', as John McKnight would say — provided a fresh perspective on who we were and what we could do. The survey process itself tightened the block, building relationships, bringing the block into living rooms and then back out.

In most every way, this city block is indistinguishable from the others. But the cumulative effect of the parties, exchange directory and other community-building activity we've engaged in makes me draw this distinction: At the very least, the neighbors on this block are *disposed* to come together and tackle big challenges as a *group*. In the 1930's, when the economy crashed, all the economic parts were in place to meet people's needs — the tractors, the factories, the trains, the workers. But the systems that connect all the parts and make it all deliver smoothly fell apart. If the systems fail again, and we're all left hanging, I can imagine my old neighbors on the other block frantically using their private telephones to get relief from various downtown agencies. But on Gallatin Street block one, I imagine one hundred and twenty people of all sizes standing together in the middle of the street, holding out their hands, vaguely in the direction of each other, and asking,

"What do we do *now?*" This is the kind of block environment I want my family to live in. A block of very different people, all gifted, who are *disposed* at the very least to come together, turn to one another, for help and support. It's a safer and more secure living environment, and it's a happier one.

Lessons

Radical isn't always dramatic. And it's not always a matter of getting to the root of a *problem*. Sometimes it's about getting to the root of what we need to do to get what we most want out of life. Block parties and consultation exchange directories don't do much, in the wider scheme of things. But efforts like these point in a *direction* of a life we might prefer to live over what we have now. They are baby steps in a direction. So, for example, on the Gallatin Street block of thirty-six households, there are four men who either live in one of the homes or regularly visit a relative or friend whom I had personally served meals and/or shelter to at the center I worked for when I moved onto the block. They made me wonder, what if our block community provided these four men the support they needed so as to dismiss their reliance on the nonprofit agencies? What if their gifts were deployed on the block and in exchange they received the support they needed? A burden shared widely enough ceases to be a burden. And what next, if we decided to roll up the paved street and created a garden, play space and block 'living room' in its place? And shared cars parked on the block's edge? What if we tried to *feed* ourselves?

The community way is radical because it represents a categorically different way of meeting needs and enjoying life than the systems we mostly depend on now that are grounded in relatively impersonal and hierarchically structured institutions and driven by the production and consumption of products, including service products. Genuine communities place members in a circle of support rather than in a pyramid powered by interpersonal competition for external rewards. Because wealth is defined in terms of relationships as well as place in a local geography, and in terms of affirmation, belonging and celebration, community systems are not inherently expansive. They present an organizational context that is conducive to human contentment as well as ecological sustainability.

Titanistad Abandon[*]

"What we might achieve, viewed from our current perspective, is not merely survival or sustainability, but paradise." — E.O. Wilson

Anything can happen, including a cultural break so deep and far-reaching it permits the earth's humans to live in harmony with each other and the planet. And it can happen within just a few decades. Such living *requires* the break, and the right break(s) may be enough to bring on the living. Easy, in the sense that culture is essentially a collective way of thinking and understanding, subject to rapid change on occasion. But this kind of change takes deliberate effort. The culture is us.

We are currently living in a Dark Age. This one is no darker in appearance than the dark ages of old, which only dimmed in hindsight. Having reached the global carrying capacity for human life on planet earth, we just might burn out from here. Dark to gone. The opposite possibility — dark to paradise — may not be less painful in the short term than complete burnout. Who knows?

[*] A version of this article was originally published as "Abandoning Ship Titanistad," *The Futurist*, July-August, 2014.

Anything can happen. Predicting burnout seems like a solid bet, examining the data and extrapolating. It is presumptuous, though, and betting on burnout is also a gratuitous waste. So is identifying and counting all the obstacles to creating a healthy and sustainable future for the world. We don't know, especially when we predict through the lens of our current cultural awareness. We're deep in our own fog.

It's like dangling from a vine off a two-hundred-foot cliff and pausing to weigh your chances of pulling yourself up to the cliff and in the same moment imagining what nasties might await you up there instead of giving your all to hoist yourself up. Paradise, or a way of life that is at least much, much better than what we have now, awaits our struggling world *as a possibility*. Our chances improve when we stop predicting and betting, shrinking into pessimism and, most of all, when we stop putting our greatest effort into keeping our McNike-Walmart-world-headed-for-burnout chugging along into the polluted sunset.

This world, our dark-age world, has been often and appropriately compared to the sinking but otherwise unsinkable ocean liner Titanic. Our culture is fascinated by this tragedy. Graft the notorious slave ship, La Amistad, to the bottom of the ocean liner and we get an even more apt sea-going metaphor: La 'Titanistad'. An unsurpassable mode of living that nevertheless requires the exploitation of most of the passengers to keep the high life humming on the upper decks. Life is miserable way down below. Harsh travelling conditions coupled with humiliation. But as the boat scrapes the iceberg, the behemoth begins to rock a bit, compromising life on all levels.

If those for whom the system is intended most to serve were ever rewarded with genuine human happiness, those rewards appear to be slipping away. Nausea on the upper decks, certainly in the middle ones. The growing discontent among those for whom the system should be working may be the hinge of cultural collapse and breakthrough. Our culture is becoming unhinged, quickly now, nowhere more obviously than in the eyes, hearts and minds of young people losing faith. Most (not all) Sixties student radicals and civil rights activists assumed a 'loyal opposition' posture in order to make the systems and structures of their world more democratic, fair and responsive to the common good generally. Though the anti-WTO, Social Forum and Occupy resistance initiatives reflect a degree of the same flavor of loyalty, many youth activists in these movements clearly do *not* share this faith, and today's comparatively less political youth just don't give a shit about the system, clearly not eager to ingest and absorb and pledge allegiance to the world their parents are feebly trying to pass on. Even the *adults* don't have confidence in the program, though the doubting may be sealed into the subconscious of many. To eke out a living, young people will go through the motions, but with little faith. This is a culture leaning on the cemetery gate.

As the North Atlantic Ocean began to fill the hulls of the Titanic, there must have been an engineer or other crew-member who became convinced that the emergency response must hop from water management to abandoning ship. Just one of the crew, while every other human on board assumed they were staying put and coping with the leak. Then the hectic conversation. A good leader is someone who can communicate bad news without overwhelming. It was likely a painful conversation. The message "get everyone in lifeboats" needed to find traction and go viral.

This is how cultural change occurs. Much like the growth pattern of our world's population, resource depletion and money supply, cultural innovation can spread at an exponential pace — slow at first, it seems, then all of a sudden, apparently. The vast, vast majority of people mimic what people around them are doing. This tendency is usually bemoaned: "People are sheep." Further, this conformity is often cited as an obstacle to change. "They'll never budge from their comfort zones."

Some Titanic passengers never did budge and went down with the ship. The first lifeboats couldn't get enough takers to fill because the 'abandon ship' virus hadn't spread sufficiently. The liner seemed so huge compared to the flimsy rafts. And the North Atlantic so cold, in the middle of nowhere. Lots of denial, and deniers. Those in charge and the premium deck passengers had more incentive to deny. That first engineer must've wondered "How can I persuade everyone on board to abandon an 'unsinkable' ship?"

But this is our challenge. The fairness of our world's systems, structures and institutions has been challenged for some time, mostly with an aim to reform rather than replace. The ecological viability of our way of life is a much more recent challenge. A world that enriches and empowers the wealthy and powerful by squeezing the life out of the poor and powerless is horrible, but can theoretically keep itself going. Our Titanistad world, however, is sinking fast by the weight of its systemic gluttony, its program no longer supported by the earth's resources. Add a growing generation gap, and we are indeed living in an end time.

Many of the passengers of the Titanic lived beyond the disaster. A very good life, I imagine, for some of the many. The first engineer who recognized the futility of saving the liner turned to his mate to share this recognition. Once the mate was sold, converting became increasingly easier. But imagine that first conversation! Once a few crewmembers were converted to lifeboating, quick and deliberate action was taken to realize the possibility that lives could be saved. If thrown overboard in dinghies, onto the icy cold North Atlantic, in the dead of night, some passengers might make it to dry land, loved ones, warmth, dry clothes. A wild utopian dream at the time?

Lessons from this disaster-as-metaphor should prove instructive for our people of the Dark Age:

1. Paradise at the other end of darkness starts with a conversation;
2. Cultural change — from "The ocean liner is safer than the lifeboats" to the opposite — precedes, as a necessary condition, behavioral change — getting in the lifeboats;
3. Once a critical mass of people change their minds and behavior, most everyone else follows along;
4. If your survival depends on the most unlikely turn of events, *go for it.*

We are the first mates. This is our conversation. On the margins there are activists busy experimenting with lifeboats. All but a few on our earth-ship, including most activists, committed to feeding or helping galley servants into mid-level cabins or perhaps take over the upper deck altogether, continue nevertheless to invest in the security of the unsinkable liner and stay on board. Spiritualists maintain their personal equilibrium by shimming the two left legs of their deck chairs, as the liner slowly tips.

What does it mean to jump ship? What *are* the lifeboats in our collapsing world? Small-scale, community-based economic networks that can survive in the absence of the global money economy, perhaps. Ways of healing, worshipping, learning, adjudicating, deciding outside the long halls of our dead or dying institutions, maybe. This requires a detailed conversation, interrupted by experiments in lifeboat living. The simpler conversation addresses our most critical and urgent question: Why must we abandon and forsake our Disneyland-SuperBowl-LasVegas-MallofAmerica extravaganza of a world, the brightest and shiniest Dark Age of all human history? Let us have — or continue having — this conversation, but also get it soon over and done with. We have paradise to build.

What We Think
Is What We Get*

I recall a Buddhist parable involving a stick that appears from a distance to be a snake, causing fear to rise in the perceiver. As the perception shifts upon closer examination, the fear subsides and the relieved hiker continues down the path. Understanding and awareness have a lot to do with how we feel and how we act. As hosts to the dominant cultural mindset (our collective understanding of who we are in the universe), our minds play a critical part in both perpetuating our dominant way of life and also in shifting away from it. And so it's just possible that I have performed no greater service in my three decades of activism than to simply challenge myself and others to consider the possibility that the social systems that support us and we sustain are inherently incapable of meeting basic human needs and that we must make a fresh start, in a sense, if we are to survive this century and prosper thereafter.

These systems are the largely invisible, cyclical patterns of interaction among and within society's individuals, institutions and principalities. They include small town school

---

* Original publication: June 15, 2009. www.swans.com

systems all the way out to our globalized economic system and
to the mother of them all, our globalized monoculture. You
need to perceive the stick as a stick before you can confidently
move on, and this consideration is a critical step in transform-
ing the way we live. When an alcoholic decides to sober up, he
needs to understand, as AA puts it, that he is powerless to the
substance. This understanding is a necessary condition for
recovery. Likewise, about six billion humans living on our
planet are powerless to make our global systems support equi-
table, sustainable, enjoyable living. Further, we are powerless
to use the tools of these systems to prevent our world from
crashing down on itself.

In a few critical ways, our global monoculture dates back to
the Mesopotamian settlements our history texts associate with
what we have labeled the Agricultural Revolution. Over the
millennia, this rapidly expanding cultural system, under the
guise of various imperial masks, has come to produce predictable results, terrible and also quite marvelous. The terrible
includes unrelieved poverty for the majority of the world's
population, widespread unhappiness and spiritual alienation,
even (especially?) among the wealthy ten percent of the
world's population, and the unsustainable use of natural
resources. This last result seals our present day ultimatum —
our culture and our survival as a species have become incompatible. As if possessing a will and mind of its own, the culture
has a voracious appetite for assimilating all cultures into itself
and then separating every thing under its umbrella from every
other thing into the smallest possible units, mainly to compete
with each other. Its compulsion is to consume and waste,
grow and expand, dominate, control and compete at a speed

and intensity that is destroying the societies we assume it has evolved to serve.

The systemic template of our civilization's form of social organization is a domination or hierarchical model, in contrast to the tribal or partnership system, which is still fully operative among isolated tribal people and recessively, in remnant forms, throughout our society. Our institutions, even small ones, are virtually all hierarchical — power, wealth and status are concentrated in individuals occupying the higher positions of a pyramidal organizational structure. In contrast, a group of friends arranging for a day together at the park is more likely to organize itself and otherwise behave in a tribal or partnership fashion. Some nuclear and even extended families exhibit partnership qualities, as do cooperatives and collectives.

Despite the predictability of what is, in other ways, a very chaotic and patchwork culture, social innovators, entrepreneurs and activists continue even in this late and desperate hour to put their best energy into trying to make this system work. Though stepping from our prevailing way of life to a better one must be done in fact and not simply in our minds, I sense that we are forestalling the necessary leap in part because too many of us remain not only actively invested in the prevailing way, but *mentally* invested as well. And there are lots of folks who at some level perceive that things have deeply soured in our world but who, like the townspeople adoring their naked emperor, keep this outlook and associated anxiety well guarded, and carry on. Indeed, though the system as a whole is failing, individuals in society are rewarded with survival goods for maximizing their effectiveness *within* the system. And just as our collective faith holds up the currency and the economy it serves, our collective faith is also what ultimately keeps civilization itself, and its supporting culture, afloat. Our active cooperation with the systems and structures of the culture is an expression of this faith.

Though I press myself into the service of partnership community building as an alternative to this, I also express through my actions a reluctant allegiance to the big culture and systems upon which my survival depends. Yet as I personally go about my daily business in life, I carry with me some fluidly changing version of the following reminders to help reorient my thinking:

1. Release your faith, Jim, in the capacity of our dominant culture, its systems and tools, to save us from social oppression, economic collapse and biological extinction. Though some of its tools (solar panels?) may be employed in the cultural hereafter, they are useful only in a marginal way in the current cultural context. Culture, as a function of how people think, understand and see the world, is the locus or hinge of social change. It is, for example, the source and determinant of technology. Promising and threatening technological advances (and potential advances) in bioengineering, fuel cells, etc., are very important, but secondary, concerns. "Keep you eyes on the prize" of cultural shift.

2. Our culture, however it serves us, is now collapsing. I can't imagine that any anthropologically trained space visitor would conclude otherwise. With each passing day,

a newborn child stands less of a chance than a child born the day before of absorbing, internalizing and embracing what the grownups need to pass on to them to assure the culture's survival. This and other factors have made for an increasingly anxious and dis-eased population. I assume that the rate of demise is of an exponential magnitude and that we're now in the 'moving very, very fast' stage. We are also destroying the habitat our biological lives depend on at a similar rate. This is a collapse on two (related) fronts.

3. Practice seeing the world as it is, in its genuine meaning, as interpreted by your most honest wits. Process attendant pain with others. Pay particular attention — honest attention — to young children. Resist writing off absurdities and horrors as normal, as business-as-usual, as just-the-way-the-world-is, as in 'toddlers/teens just behave that way'. Allow yourself to witness and feel the effects of a desperate and dying culture.

4. It may be possible to stop or even prevent a war, move more poor people into affordable housing or to make a nonpolluting car. Efforts like these are necessary. Keep making them, but also keep in mind that while they cushion systemic blows and enhance the lives of individuals (perhaps millions of them), these measures will not directly alter our cultural or systemic trajectories. If you teach a child to read in school, or campaign for school reform or more public expenditures for the school system, keep a third eye as you go on a not too distant future in which children, as fully reintegrated members of their communi-

ties, learn, grow and become strong, healthy adults in some manner very different from what they experience in today's institutional settings.

5. Try to be a responsible, centered, loving person. It's good for you and the world. But while bad people exacerbate social problems, they are not the problems. Likewise, good people are not the solutions. Though individuals make consequential choices, systems rule for the most part. The force of our dominant culture — as a system itself — and the many social, economic and political systems flowing within it drive and shape much of what we do, how we live and even many of the smallest choices we make. Car driving, as an example, is a terribly polluting, resource depleting, unhealthy, violent and isolating activity, but at the same time — and on another level — it is a very rational, life sustaining practice performed routinely by good people everywhere. Invisible systemic forces within the flow of our culture, and the structural manifestations of these forces, compel it. We will therefore have to change the cultural flow, create systems that work for people generally as they are. We will never get our current systems to work by trying to make people in them better, as many of us have been struggling to do. Look to see (and change) systems more and blame (credit or change) individuals less.

6. Unlike physical systems, the social systems that shuttle us around, as powerful as they are, are also paper-thin. They are vulnerable to change, even rapid, dramatic change. They have structural and material manifestations that

seem overwhelmingly formidable, but our social systems are ultimately sustained through the sponsorship of our minds. This principle was demonstrated in the collapse of the Soviet Union in 1991, an effect of a private conversation that snowballed into a movement with irrepressible force.

7. Have faith that people can live equitably, sustainably and happily and that we are ambitious and inventive enough to fully recreate the way we live. 'Where there is a will there is a way' applies. Generating will requires awareness. For sure, we are facing a profound social and psycho-spiritual challenge associated with cultural collapse and transformation. Humans are also stunningly adaptable. People are stuck, tethered to the dominant system, but as we become aware that our cultural Titanistad is really going down, enough people will scramble to invent and to cut paths for others to follow. One method our culture uses to bolster our faith in it is to convince us that we can't live any other way:

- We're not good enough (starting with a belief in innate depravity).
- It's up to the people in power to make big change.
- The weight of change itself is too heavy (as if it's all on my plate).
- Or, there simply is no viable, even thinkable, alternative to the basic competitive, hierarchical framework we've been living under.

Confront and challenge these familiar mantras as they creep into your mental projections.

8. Look out for and pay attention to forward-reaching experiments. For some time, cultural innovators have been trying to experiment a way out of the dominant mode of living. Many of these social experiments are small, perhaps even conventional-looking trials. Many fail, which is par for the course of change. In trying to assess an experiment in this regard, ask yourself, 'Does this experiment point to a world, say ten or twenty years out, that I would want to live in if the experiment were to succeed?' I would cite Gaviotas, of rural Columbia (*www.friendsofgaviotas.org*), and the Dudley Street Neighborhood Initiative, of Boston (*www.dsni.org*), as two large-scale examples that inspire this kind of change. Catch yourself dismissing outright any person or group trying or saying something strange and different, then lend support to those pointing to a world you really want for you and our children.

9. Don't get stuck on, or worry over, what the world or your part of it is going to look like or how everything is going to fit together once the cultural dust settles. Contemplating 'What if?' and 'How are we going to?' scenarios might itself be the biggest obstruction. We *have* to move forward and out of where we are. A mass redeployment of creative energy and focus, driven by cultural shift, will produce results that are unimaginable to us now. 'Necessity is the mother of invention.' Internalize the necessity.

10. The dominant cultural vision is not one of global diversity, but global assimilation. It imagines every person living essentially the same way, speaking the same language, trading in the same currency at the same store. Assume that creating a new way of life in the ashes of this vision will be closer to creating new *ways* of life. The tribal/partnership system has a very good and long track record as a basic form of social organization for humans, and:

  a) this form allows for genuine cultural diversity and countless ways of living beyond the basic form;

  b) people may invent civilizational forms that work in ways our current form doesn't; and

  c) there are options and possibilities other than these two basic forms.

11. As you free your thinking in these ways and relieve yourself of the burden — in your mind at least — of trying to make our systems work, encourage others to do the same and link up with an experiment in progress and/or innovate yourself. *But even if you make no outward change in your life*, this perspective shift will bring us significantly closer to a much, much better world, especially if you risk a conversation now and then. How we perceive and how we think are powerful forces of change.

12. Find likeminded people to support and to support you. There are millions of people suffering various kinds and degrees of oppression and desperation as they try, often in isolation, to negotiate our troubled world. When hands

and minds are joined and we begin to see that the source of our trouble isn't located in us, only some of the symptoms, we create a bond with enormous potential for change. 'Where there are two or more gathered' for this kind of conversation and mutual support, anything can grow from it. There is a 'tipping point' somewhere in this social transformation and your small contribution is very likely a needed one. As such, it is also a decisive one.

I have to honestly think of myself as deeply cynical and hopeless in relation to what I believe our cultural systems and institutions can ultimately provide us. A new deal with the old dealers won't save us. New dealers in the same game won't either. A new game, or an assortment of new games, might. The needed change is fundamentally a cultural change, not a piece of legislation or a piece of technology, and it is a change that is struggling from many directions to break through. Conditioned to see newsmaking individuals, institutions and events — not systems — this cultural shifting is relatively invisible and underreported. Have faith in it, be on the look out and maybe even jump in somewhere.

Deep Bullshit

A victim of bullshit exposure, I suppose, I can't quite bring myself to believe that there is a capital 'T' truth that is either embedded in the universe and/or present in the mind of a supernatural being. Still, I'm compelled by Professor Harry G. Frankfurt's bestseller distinctions between truth telling, lying and 'bullshitting', which, a greater evil than lying, according to Frankfurt, refers to various forms of self-promotional blather let go without regard for the truth of its content.[*] As a social change activist troubled by the direction our world is heading in today, I want to affirm the critical importance of carefully sifting through the pile of pronouncements and other information that is spooned into our brains every day. It is not an academic exercise. In the spirit of extending the professor's sifting mission to a field in which the 'bullshitter' is our dominant culture, impersonal and (as such) innocent, rather than a manipulative, self-serving person or institution, I share some of my own findings. The cultural assumptions presented here are interconnected, having evolved into a semi-coherent web — or tapestry — of deep bullshit.

[*] Harry G. Frankfurt, *On Bullshit.* Princeton, N.J.: Princeton University Press, 2005.

"Economic security is having lots of money, or at least a reliable source of lots of money" is bullshit. Now, the truth of this matter, assuming one, cannot be something narrow and superficial. I do not dispute that individuals with lots of money enjoy economic security in the short-term, or that impoverished families struggling to feed themselves will be rewarded by securing a reliable income. But all this is about financial, not economic security, in truth. Nowadays people know, at least in a vague way, what is meant when someone predicts that "the global financial system will collapse soon." About two years ago, many economists (wholly out of character) were speaking in these terms. At the very least, the system continues to teeter, precariously sustained on a money-printing drip feed. Alternatively, an economic system that depends on a reliable and trustworthy community of people and a familiar land base is vulnerable pretty much to meteors and other catastrophic acts of nature. In this regard, while the tenured, Ivy League faculty member, as such, enjoys a very high level of *financial security* among Americans, the Amish farmer, as such, enjoys a very high level of *economic* security. The successful Wall Street Ponzi schemer may sit atop a much taller mountain of dough, but is much less secure than either the farmer or the professor. The money-based, global economy we have created is not a *false* economy, because it *does* provide, but it is a *bullshit* economy, because it is built on abstract versions of the foundational conditions upon which real, sustainable economies are built. The next item here might clarify the distinction between the bullshit economy of our global financial system and a truer economy.

"We are running out of time" is bullshit. People throughout the civilized world, meaning just about everybody, organize much of their lives (depending on their proximity to civilization's urban centers) on the basis of time measurement devices and the time they measure. Civilization builders created the concept of time we measure with evermore finely calibrated clocks in order to synchronize the movement of an increasingly large number of humans living closer and closer together. The rest of earth life, and also primitive and other outlying humans, rely on nature's cycles and rhythms to navigate their movement. Like our financial system, time as we know it is real on a certain level, and certainly functional as a basis for coordinating our steps, but it is essentially a bullshit version of cycles and rhythms (nature's way). To eat when it's dinnertime, not when hungry, to sleep when it's bedtime, not when tired, to learn when the bell rings, not when compelled to investigate, is bullshit, when you think about it. Humans in civilization, imagining in their evolving worldview that 'nature' is something distinct, something, in particular, distinct from themselves, enabled the invention of their culture's bullshit version of cycles and rhythms. The clock tells us when to go places and do things. It has also become our prison cell.

"I am British" is bullshit. Like our financial system and clock time, political borders and identities are bullshit versions of geological and cultural boundaries. Shifting and porous as they often are, boundaries structure the natural world, and they structure tribal people still living in the wild. Young children living in our bordered world intuit the fakeness of our political borders and must be conditioned to recognize and honor their legitimacy. Allegiance is transferred from a culture, usually receding in our world under the force of assimilation to the dominant culture, to a nation. "I am British" is certainly not meaningless or completely untrue, but it is bullshit, more basically.

"**I own this house**" is passable as true as far as it goes, but of course this claim, related to border claims generally, implies this deeper bullshit claim: "I own the land my house sits on." Land certainly is real, but claiming to own 'real property' is baseless other than on the very practical level related to the collective need to preserve the commons (and there are certainly other ways of accomplishing this). But the conception of land ownership devised by our culture over the centuries consists in a *moral* claim, as in a natural or moral or human right, and this claim is recognized, supported and enforced by states everywhere. In our world, the ultimate and only real basis of land ownership, hidden behind the moral claim mask, is brute force — the ability to militarily defend the geography inside the fence you erect around it. 'Might makes right' is the only non-bullshit stab at a moral claim justifying ownership. The child (who must be bullshitted into an adult, as a large patch of her education) doesn't see the distinction between owning a plot of land and the absurdity of owning the sky, or the ocean, or the moon.

"**Children attend school to learn and develop into resourceful adults**" is bullshit. Not entirely false, this is a seldom-challenged assumption in our culture more than a claim, and it is supported by evidence that learning and personal growth are associated with schooling. They are even a *result*, clearly, of school experience in many instances. But you can also make progress cutting timbers with a butter knife. A good, partially serrated butter knife can penetrate the bark, maybe cut in a bit further, but it's not the proper tool for the job. Shifting metaphors only slightly, Derrick Jensen generalizes that children are to students what trees are to two by fours. On the other hand, schools have proven to be a reasonably effective mechanism for keeping children from underfoot in the adult-centered world of work and to condition future workers to adjust to and produce for our remarkably school-like work environments. The world itself is the more appropriate vehicle for learning and personal growth. In human communities where kids are still permitted in — or are not excluded from — the living world of adults and trees, the young ones learn and grow much more easily and also more freely.

"I work in that office building" is clearly not a lie, unless the speaker really doesn't work there. Like the other examples above, however, this innocent claim sits atop the sad bullshit distinction we make in our culture between 'going to work' (like 'going to learn') and 'living'. When remote tribal people, like the Hadza of the Tanzanian bush country, are followed by anthropologists wanting to test the old saw that primitive people must constantly struggle to survive in the raw environment, the researchers have found that the 'work' day is actually closer to half the length of ours, or a mere four hours of 'work' per day. This finding is very useful to dispel the myth about tribal workaholism, but of course the finding must be qualified by the matter of fact that the Hadza do not 'work' at all. Lunch is indeed free for them. Getting it requires 'work', as physics uses the term (an expenditure of energy), but always in a manner that is woven into the fabric of living day to day. To work at one moment, in a specified place, to learn at another specified time in a very different place, and so on with recreation and the rest of our activity, constitutes bullshit fragmentation. This is one way we are — together — bullshitting our way through life.

"Son, we get food by paying for it at the supermarket." True on one level, of course, this explanation is a common line of bullshit. As young children, most of us learn where milk comes from, besides the store. But as adults, we are so far removed from the sources of our food — even what our food *is* — that we are wandering the aisles in bullshitland as far as our connection to real food goes. Food is absolutely *central* to the survival and wellbeing of all living organisms, including people. Yet we the people of our culture have drifted first from any direct connection to the sources of our food, then subsequently from real food itself, as we've drifted insidiously to eating food-like commodities that are basically bullshit food. In it there may be foodlike nutrients and other properties present, but as 'food', it's bullshit.

*****

The global culture of our global world has been the font of boundless creativity and much that is beautiful and life affirming. But we have also been building the house of our world, now global in its reach and scale, on a mound of bullshit. The foundational assumptions identified above are among countless others (like the culturally constructed 'adolescence' purgatory) that collectively undergird the systemic architecture of our bullshit culture. The cultural pieces — clocks and borders, for examples — fit clumsily together and mutually reinforce one another in a manner that works for us on some levels, but the whole of it makes for a world that is out of control, out of balance, out of whack, oppressive and disempowering for most people, a world that is literally out of touch with the earth and its nonnegotiable systems.

For those who are either unsettled by this disconnect or who experience daily some form of oppression generated by it, there is a lesson that can be as liberating as it is discouraging: There is no viable way to be free within the pile of shit. We must cut through, dig ourselves out, get out. We have to adopt a vision — or visions — that extend beyond our culture in order simply to survive much longer on the planet. Things will keep failing and falling apart if we continue to assume that the basic way we presently think and live together are immutable. This is the sobering piece of the lesson. The more freeing piece is recognizing the genuine opportunity before us to think and live in very different ways. Trails are being cut by creative and passionate people around the globe, but most of the cutting and creating is being detained by the grip of our cultural assumptions governing the perceived parameters of change. The bullshit is our shared delusions. What will happen when we let them go?

One Less Car
on the Road*

S
he knew it would fit. And she knew me as well as anyone did. In big letters on the back, the T-shirt read 'ONE LESS CAR ON THE ROAD'. A crusading environmentalist biking alone past hundreds of motor vehicles stuck in traffic, a moving billboard: 'ONE LESS CAR ON THE ROAD'. With politeness and gratitude for the thought, I declined the gift.

I passed on the prospect of being hollered and honked at, or worse. Just adds to the peril. Deeper, though, the shirt and message presents a distorted picture of both the problem and the solution in the too-many-cars department. The underlying assumption is that individual behaviors are the problem and also that individual behavioral *change* is the solution. This assumption is OK, on a level, but of very limited use. Clearly and more specifically, the message implies that the environmental crisis is partially reducible: a) to the ignorance and/or insensitivity of car drivers (the problem); and b) to "why don't you park your SUV and bike like me, nooneyhead?" (the solution).

*   Original publication: "One Less Car on the Road," *Population Press*, July 1, 2014.

I bike for many reasons. It supports good health, I'm out in the open, freer to experience the environment (crappy and beautiful) and wave to friends, who can see me. Parking is convenient. Biking is very energy efficient and very clean. It is also less expensive — or quicker — than car driving, by either type of measurement: time or money. This rationale needs elaboration. I average around twelve miles per hour in the city. On average, a typical, single car owner travels somewhere between four and nine mph on average when all the purchase and maintenance expenses associated with the car are converted to the owner's time working a job to get the money. Then actually *driving* the car takes more time (and money and then more time) at the gym and/or doctor's office. Pretty slow, all totaled. And then there's huge pollution and resource depletion costs, collectively incurred. Car driving isolates people. Roads divide communities, plaster the earth, allow toxified water to run right into rivers. Over thirty thousand Americans die each year from car accidents. Even wars and military preparedness expenses should be factored in. Very hazardous. If all car owners had to absorb all the collective costs as well as their personal car expenses, they'd find themselves driving in reverse most of the time. Though a good bike tire is expensive, the cost in money, converted to hours, to support my bike habit doesn't even slow me down to eleven mph.

With climate control features, car driving is more comfortable than the bike, however, and biking may not be any safer (for the *biker*) so long as cars far outnumber cyclists and otherwise rule the road. That's, however, about it.

Despite all the good reasons to bike rather than drive, it's wholly inadequate and dangerously beside the point to blame or lecture the drivers (especially since many cyclists like me drive plenty as well!). Our culture relentlessly conditions us to notice and prioritize individuals and institutions and to assume that the isolated behavior of these agents can explain our problems in full. Systems thinking, in contrast, looks *between* and *around* individuals, institutions and events for patterns of *systemic* behavior. Seeing and understanding systems and the power they have to shape and drive what we do can make individual behavior much more understandable and predictable. And also forgivable, if and when forgiveness is necessary or appropriate.

Drivers — and their passengers — drive because the flow of our systems (a torrent really) *compels* us to drive. Our economic system, structures and patterns very nearly require car driving in all but a few places. The shortage of reliable mass transit is part of this pressure, but the incentives to drive run much deeper: government subsidies to oil, infrastructure, and car companies; where we (have to) work; the work we do; and the location of stores, especially food stores. The forces of globalization, though permitting many to work from home, also lure many to move unbikable distances. In the US in particular, self-contained communities, walkable and bikable, are relics of a slower past.

By all powers, go ahead and bike. It's better, on balance. The personal and collective benefits of one more cyclist on the road accrue with each convert. Good. But campaigning to get individuals to buck the systemic flow and cycle is an insufficient solution to our environmental or social crises. Changing the flow is a more promising alternative. We start with the reality that the vast, vast, vast majority of us more or less do what the other people around us are doing. Nearly everyone of us are good at adding our bodies neatly to the end of a line of other lined-up people, even when it just *seems* to be heading in the direction we want. We herd well, go with the flow. Humans are often chided for our sheepishness. "If only we can break people out of the driving habit (and bike seven miles down Route 1 to work everyday), we're so lazy!" OK, on one level, we are lazy and, it surely seems, becoming lazier. But there's no changing people in this regard in any direct or immediate fashion. Maybe one or two, usually for short time periods. It's not the laziness we have to account for as much as the conformity.

The brighter side of the conformity coin is that we are all just as likely to adopt *positive* habits so long as the systemic flow is with us and enough people have adopted. Create systems and structures that make walking and biking (or mass transit) the paths of least resistance for getting round and ordinary people with the usual mix of virtues and vices will stop driving. Something close to this describes cities like Boston and New York, still choked with car traffic, but also filled with residents who don't drive, for reasons of convenience more than holiness.

It's difficult to overstate how disposed the people of our culture are to lean on individuals and institutions to blame for social problems and also to solve them. The CEO of one of the biggest banks reportedly confessed in the wake of the '08 crash that he was well aware that his bank's reckless investment frenzy was pushing the economy to the brink, but that he couldn't help participating in and thereby reinforcing the frenzy. His competitors were in it full tilt, his bank was raking in the green and anyway he would quickly be replaced if he applied the brakes. No excuse? Yes, on a personal level, no excuse. There is a box within which personal accountability is very real and very meaningful. But outside the box of personal ethics, the CEO — and the rest of us — were pawns of a systemic tragedy. Clearly, our economic system selects for greed, so acquisitive types are rewarded and rise to positions of power and wealth. Our economic system also *must grow simply to maintain itself.* Put these systemic features together and bubbles such as we experience (bigger these days, and more frequent) are highly predictable. The exponential growth of our money supply begged for all the accumulated dough to get busy somewhere, somehow, *anywhere, anyhow.* This systemic necessity compelled the invention of impenetrably complex and risky investment tools, lending money to anyone in any manner.

The "too much greed" chorus doesn't cut very deeply into the crisis, looked at this way. Only slightly more systemic-minded are those who blame lax oversight and regulation. But given the pressure to grow and invest, the laxity itself was predictable. In a system, the *parts self-organize,* or dance with each other, to serve the aim of the system (like growth), and generally the parts choreograph themselves with remarkably little awareness of the total effect. Certainly, tighter oversight of investment practices and regulating policies would manage the frenzy some. But the fact that, as of this writing, the

Federal Reserve is lending 2.8 billion each *day* of fresh new dollars into the economy to keep a recession from dropping down into depression suggests that solving the crisis will require more than policy change and firmer oversight.

*****

The world is deeply indebted to Mahatma Gandhi for demonstrating the power of nonviolent resistance in overthrowing British rule in India. But his greater contribution to the social and ecological crises of both his day and ours is arguably his "Constructive Program," his insistence on creating sustainable, local, very small scale economies. Many thinkers and doers since Gandhi (and before him) have developed theoretical frameworks and practical tools for redirecting the systemic flow that has been flushing us all into greater inequality, insecurity, and ecological ruin on a global level. Clearly, failure to adequately redirect the current flow could spell the end of humanity in the near term, but the promise of the global 're-localization' movement lies primarily in its systemic orientation. More precisely, this movement is more radical than prior liberation and libertarian movements because of how it contextualizes the essential roles large scale political and economic institutions play in sustaining the global industrial growth system. Yet relocalization is not ideological in any traditional sense. Old-fashioned, ancient, and indigenous wisdom and life skills are being plied into a variety of new experiments in community economics: small groups of people, bound to each other as equals and to their local geography, supporting each other to meet basic needs before selling their 'comparative advantage' surplus to the wider community or a network of communities.

For obvious reasons, relocalization is anything but a global, centralized movement. There is, for example, no unified rejection of large institutions or political regimes that might continue in some capacity to serve small communities and networks of communities. But the primary unit is the community, not the state or corporation. It *does* translate into a dramatic systemic shift in how we structure our lives. It will mean travelling less in general, and travelling shorter distances. And less driving.

Systems scientist Donella Meadows emphasized that the prime mover in systemic change is not the action itself of creating change, but the mindset, or paradigm, that powers and informs it. There's no way around changing minds, in other words, to change systems. Public policy mandates forcing top down behavioral change that lasts can be effective mostly to the extent to which the coerced behavior becomes habit-forming and changes thinking over time. Upon seizing power in 1949, the communist regime in China outlawed the foot binding of women, among many other cultural practices deemed abusively archaic. States in the U.S. mandated recycling. Political revolutions and policy reforms change thinking through changing behavior, relying on coercion and good citizenship. Propaganda campaigns that accompany coercion, such as the DUI initiative in the U.S., reflect the need to change thinking to change behavior long term. It can work, but effective policy can never get too far ahead of popular culture, as the pathetic results of so many legal mandates such as alcohol and drug use prohibition demonstrate (In these instances, a culture of addiction pushes addictive behavior, the reality of personal decision-making and responsibility notwithstanding).

More deeply, the massive shift to relocalize is simply not likely to unfold in this way. And so far it hasn't. Local government initiatives (notably in cities such as Copenhagen, San Francisco, Curitiba, Brazil, and Ogawamachi, Japan) have shown that government can play a vital role in re-empowering local, sustainable economies. Otherwise, thousands of conversations, starting with two people, have spawned thousands of promising alternatives to globalization worldwide that center on creating local, community-based economies. In my state of Rhode Island, there is a rapidly growing local food production and distribution system. Internationally, small groups of people have created over a thousand 'Transition Initiatives' to reclaim their own labor and local resources. In Auroville, India; Faoune, Senegal and many other communities around the world, communitarian eco-villages have experimented with localized alternatives to the global economy.

Relocalizing our personal and economic lives is an example of a systems thinking departure from the tendency to rely on comparatively unrealistic aspirations for either individual betterment at one end and government policy solutions at the other. Learning to see, understand and respect the power of systemic behavioral patterns and traps (once established, systems tend to generate their own behavior) amounts itself to a mindset change that enables structural innovations, including relocalization efforts. Additionally, relocalization recognizes that the global, industrial growth economy now supporting us is unreliable and unsustainable and must be displaced, that viable alternatives must answer to our deep human need to belong in community and connect to our land base, that our culture's individualism is a bloated caricature of authentic individuality, and that we are connected to, not separate from or above each other and the earth.

As author Daniel Quinn insists, a change in cultural vision this deep has the power and know-how to transform systems, structures and behavior with*out* programs, as we've come to know and rely on them. Still, most adopters of this change can and may grow into the evolving cultural vision as they settle into new living patterns carved out by others. Activists leading change need to recognize and appreciate that there is no shortcut around this deep complexity in building a just and sustainable world, but also that this 'long haul' approach may produce surprisingly quick results. In a world addicted to solitary motoring to get around, converting drivers one by one into cyclists will take much more time than we have.

I Had a Martin Luther King Dream[*]

On an early May morning, 2014, I was fast asleep in a room in a house atop a mountain on the western edge of the Mojave Desert. There and then I had a dream. The otherwise busy dream featured a brief but vivid shouting match between me and Martin Luther King. No mistaking it was King. I was vaguely aware of what I was excited to share with my teacher (we never met in waking life), but the exchange did not last beyond this:

> Me: "I have something to tell you!" [delivered with some enthusiastic intensity]
>
> Martin: "*No, you* listen to *me!*" [with escalated intensity]
>
> Me: "No, you don't under*stand!*" [holding the intensity]
>
> Martin: "No, *you* don't understand!" [escalating a bit]

Then Martin seamlessly vanished into the ether of the dream, which carried on with no apparent connection to this encounter (besides, stretching a lot, my brother-in-law and I noticing the high ocean tide gently lapping against the back of our beach house). It isn't any more characteristic of me to engage

---
[*] Original publication: February 28, 2015. www.jesusradicals.com

in such substanceless shouting matches as it was of MLK. I recall, in the dream, *wanting* to sit down and have a certain dialogue, but he just let into me (of course, this is *my* reporting of the event!). In his response, no doubt, there is a message for me. But in the dream analysis meantime, I will settle for sharing, in a letter, the thought I was so excited to have the chance to run by Martin, but could not:

Dear Martin,

I sometimes wonder how Jesus would've responded if he and his disciples happened upon one of those small isolated, ungoverned, uncivilized bands of people we used to call, until very recently, 'savages'. Are you aware of any encounter like this that actually — or might have — occurred? During his ministry, all continents were home to tribal people of whom he could not have been aware. Nor could he have been aware that his human ancestors, presumably living in small band communities, roamed and settled on every continent for tens of thousands of years before his time, and before that, roamed and settled on his own side of the planet for millions of years. All struggling to meet the survival challenges of life in Earth, yet free of the oppression of empire, and finding ways to live suitably with themselves and the Earth.

"The poor will always be with us" was an impressive retort to the disciples who resisted the devoted woman anointing Jesus' feet with expensive oils, but it would not have occurred to Jesus to substitute the more historically correct "The poor will always be with empire and civilization." These structures were fully entrenched in his world; impossible to see beyond their historical or geo-anthropological horizons to the vast expanse of human living without the poverty known to Jesus and to us (Columbus, it has been said in many ways, did not *discover* poverty in the New World, he *created* it).

What message would he attempt to deliver to the tribes-people? Or inquiries? What observations? Would he at some early point turn to his own band and say, "Go, disciples, and live like these people after I am no longer with you. Spread the word and example that others may follow." If he were lucky, he and his disciples would have been shown the finest hospitality (most likely from the very isolated, 'untouched' tribes). Or, they may have had to run for their lives (among some tribes that had had bad experience with the civilized). It has been said that Jesus disappointed the Zealots and other Hebrew liberationists by refusing to take interest in challenging Roman rule, perhaps replacing it with a (more) righteous empire. My suggestion, Martin, is that Jesus signaled something more radical, yet not otherworldly radical: to walk away from empire altogether, to live (politically) ungoverned, and, yes, uncivilized, in small, egalitarian communities of people dedicated to supporting each other, within their means, from cradle to grave, living sustainably off, by and within their local land base, with a degree of trial and error (as is the way of evolution). "We've lost our tribal roots, people."

The New Testament Book of Acts reports the apostles of Jesus trying to find these roots and create this community. The eschatological backdrop behind this communitarian response does not diminish the significance of choosing this particular manner of waiting on their Lord's return. "All who believed were together and had all things in common and they sold their possessions and goods and distributed them to all, as any had need." (Acts 1:44-5; RSV) In more recent times, or perhaps ever since, Christian ministry has prioritized service — helping others, the needy, generally those outside one's own immediate community — over community building itself. Miraculous healings notwithstanding, Jesus was a community builder, wasn't he Martin? The potential of a church *community* was expressed in the power of the civil rights movement under your pastoral leadership.

There's nothing especially perfect about the Yequana Indians of the Amazon or the San tribes of Southern Africa, the Sng'oi of Malaysia, but they don't need Jesus, especially, *do* they? What the Apostles attempted to create for themselves in an instant these indigenous people cobbled together over many centuries. 'Tribal' refers simply to a form of social organization, no more romantic or barbaric or controversial than lions organizing themselves in 'prides' or whales in 'pods'. It's a form that has worked well for humans over hundreds of thousands of years. Each tribe features a different culture, developed over generations in response to (changing) environmental conditions — opportunities and challenges. The tribal form roughly consists of a small group of people, related more or less as equals (in contrast most clearly to our hierarchies), whose bases of support are each other's energy and gifts, and the surrounding land base. The *content* of this basic form can differ dramatically between tribes. We notice these differences, many of which we find disturbing, more than we appreciate the basic tribal form. Sounds to me what Jesus lived and preached. What do you think? I'm curious to know because your thinking was so expansive, always challenging and on the move. Your "Beyond Vietnam" speech remains the most powerfully succinct critique of U.S involvement there I have read. Might something like this, some stepping out 'beyond civilization', be your next challenge, though many of your colleagues will reject or dissuade you, as they did over Vietnam? Is it not perhaps civilization itself, beyond the empire of the moment, that is the world's "greatest purveyor of violence" and oppression?

The tribal way continues today, now in geographically isolated spaces, but also recessively within our own globalizing world (Alcoholics Anonymous comes to mind). The comparatively recent emergence of civilizations marked a departure from tribal living, experimental initiatives to improve life. The Mesopotamian origins and early expansion of Western Civilization are chronicled in Genesis, though the account is reported as the birth of *humanity*, interestingly, not of civilization. There were lots of other people living there in Eden, Martin, unnoticed or dismissed by the chroniclers. Nothing especially perfect about them or their way of life, rough and tumble, but *connected* to and with the rest of the community of life there. Making a living, integrated. Eating the fruit from the knowledge tree calls out a particular tribe and people, one among the thousands of Garden dwellers, who plunged into engineering their lives by a set of rules that would position them as superior to and rulers of the other earth's creatures, including the remaining human tribes. The most you could say for the Creator's reaction to this bold adventure is that He had mixed feelings.

This self-positioning — humans over the rest of life — not only permitted and encouraged the self-aggrandizing rape of the planet, but also the emergence of racism. As the conquering civilization expanded, the lighter-skinned conquerors began to distinguish themselves by this physical marker from the darker-skinned tribal people encountered along the way. The conquered were lesser both outside and then, assimilated, inside the empire. The 'power over' structure of empire makes racism essentially systemic, not, essentially, personal or even institutional. Within the domain of our civilization's culture, prejudice, bigotry, even discrimination can go both ways, are reversible, but racism cannot and is not. Consequently, the effects of racism can be cushioned, but racism can never be substantially removed from the systemic core of civilizational culture.

Jesus called on his people to abandon this project, not to replace the Roman Empire, but empire itself, civilization itself. There's nothing more antithetical to Jesus' life and message than an Egyptian pyramid, symbol of our civilization (featured even today on the U.S. dollar bill). Wealthy, powerful, lighter-skinned men at the top sucking power and wealth and status from the foundational masses, and the earth itself, holding it all up.

"Render unto Caesar what belongs to Caesar" was not a suggestion to pay taxes to the empire, but to surrender *all* its money. And then walk away. The command was an expression of faith. If the arc of the moral universe bends toward justice, the arc does not pass through empire, through imperial systems, structures, institutions, through civilization itself, no. At least not ours. No faith in these, Jesus.

The "birds of the air and the flowers of the field" he called us to emulate. In nature's systems, abundance is accessible to those with limited wants. Living this way is 'uncivilized' indeed. 'Civilized' means idealizing making lots of stuff and buying lots of stuff. This 'fever pitched' lifestyle was rejected by your other teacher, Socrates, in *The Republic* (Book II, 372-4), before his sometime loyal student, Plato, coaxed him into defining 'justice' for humans on the terms of civilization, which features unlimited wants and regular mass warfare. Living in the wild, tribal people forage and hunt, like the birds. We civilized must find and keep a job, grovel for the pyramidal money and purchase our way to survival.

Even by "turning the other cheek" and "carrying the soldier's pack an extra mile," disciples were urged to resist, not support, empire. Both are acts of nonviolent defiance of arbitrary authority, like the taking of blows by freedom riders and demonstrators and lunch counter customers. How could a Roman soldier handle an insistent offer to carry his pack an extra mile when the emperor's own rule limited such conscription to a single mile?

I know I'm cherry-picking my gospel references here, Martin, and interpreting them. We all do it, though — paste together our impression of the 'real' Jesus. But doesn't this resemble *your* Jesus? During my forty years of activism, I have supported, participated in and occasionally led social justice efforts. I support them today. Not sure this — my, your — Jesus would, and I find that personally challenging, every day. The pyramid can soften a little toward inclusivity, to democracy, to equal opportunity and social mobility. These adjustments, having a lot to do with preserving the system (FDR insisted he had saved Capitalism, not destroyed it with his progressive New Deal programs), are what we have called 'justice'. It's a very low bar, no?

Where and what is the promise land on this planet? Tell me it isn't the marginalized and oppressed, the stone draggers, gaining traction in the pyramid, or even taking the pyramid over and redistributing its wealth and freedom and power. The Zealots must've hoped for the latter in some fashion, Jesus leading the revolution. Without replacing the cultural thinking supporting civilization, and the silent assumption that civilization is a non-negotiable, any realigned pyramid will reshape itself in short order to its preferred hierarchical form. As it has.

What does it mean to walk away, to defect, from civilization? Does it mean acknowledging its failure as an experimental alternative to the time-tested tribal way, and retribalizing (in new ways, presumably, appropriate to our current circumstances)? Like the rest of us, Jesus was taught to believe that Genesis was the story of humanity's beginning, not our transition to civilization and empire. So perhaps, seeing into the hearts and minds and bodies of his richly diverse Eden-dwelling brothers and sisters, he might simply put it this way — cut our losses in the pyramid and retribalize. Or maybe 'walking away' looks very different — some third way between or beyond both tribalism and civilization in their various shades and colors.

Where do we go, Martin, from here?

Yours in dreamland,

Jim

Falling into slumber tonight, and on successive nights, I will pray for a reply. Good night!

Shall the Poor Always
Be with Us?*

I t was a righteous and otherwise innocent enough reply
to the disciples who took offense at the faithful
woman's lavish 'waste' of expensive perfume on their
master. Jesus clearly did not pretend by his remark to be
shedding new light on the problem of poverty. And when we
remind ourselves, as we so often do, that "the poor will always
be with us" (as they always *have* been), we are merely borrow-
ing a manner of stating a fact we all accept without a second
thought. It was a fact as unquestioned in Jesus' time as it is
today. But it is not exactly a *fact* about the poor — that they
always have been (and always will be) with us. It is one of
those collectively held assumptions that constitute the mythology of our culture, the culture of what has become our
global civilization.

It is not an idle myth, that the poor will always be with us, but
a *vital* myth, a powerful and essential means of sustaining our
culture and the business of it as usual. It is a myth that has
haunted me throughout my two and a half decades of feeling
and actively expressing both compassion and indignation in

---

* A version of this essay first appeared in *The Other Side*, Vol. 38, No. 3,
May-June 2002.

relation to the persistence of hunger, homelessness and poverty in our affluent nation and abroad. Most of this time I
spent working at Amos House, a soup kitchen and homeless
shelter, trying, I suppose, to escape my own affluence and
privilege as well as meet basic human needs and challenge the
political powers.

The cultural 'purpose' of the myth is as clearly straightforward
as it is debilitating to the caring activist: there's no sense in
trying to *end* poverty, except in our dreams. The dreams are
reflected in our rhetoric, but under the surface we realize that
the prize we can reasonably strive for is amelioration.

Consider, on the other hand, that poverty as we know it is
not and has never been the fate of humanity, but instead is
largely a product of civilization, as we know it. Columbus and
other European explorers and colonists, for example, did
not discover poverty here in the Americas; they created it.
Defined in terms of security, control and access to life-
sustaining resources, poverty and affluence take on a meaning
apart from our conventional 'standard of living' measure. This
reinterpretation prompted anthropologist Marshall Sahlins
thirty years ago to identify tribal hunter-gatherers as the
"original affluent societies." He recognized a kind of wealth
enjoyed — and enjoyed *equitably* — by tribal people that far
surpassed in value the benefits we associate with having
wealth in our culture. Perhaps because we have begun to
change our own conventional measures of wealth, hunter-
gatherers are beginning to be perceived by us in a more favor-
able light. My students do generally pause to consider if the

Native Americans were 'poor' when encountered by European explorers, but then uniformly insist that they were not.

And although scientists discovered over a century ago that humans lived in this hunter-gatherer way for hundreds of thousands of years before the Agricultural Revolution spawned our civilization and culture a mere ten thousand years ago, our history and our collectively held and lived mythology reduce the human experience to civilization building. Our collective frame of reference not only omits the vast human experience prior to our history, it excludes the experience of humans flourishing in egalitarian tribes *concurrent* with our history. There are still today scattered pockets of tribal people who have never known the kind of poverty we take so for granted. This vast experience suggests that poverty is a function of culture, not of nature, which is relatively immutable.

So one way we perpetuate the myth of never-ending poverty is by continuing to believe, against the facts, that *our* history, the history of *our* culture, *our* civilization is the history of humanity itself and that anyone outside or predating this history is a poor, half-human savage. Many of us individually will nod to the facts when confronted by them. This matters little, because mythology is something a culture of people buy into *together* and gives expression to in the way they live *as a group*.

In the same vein, a second and more recent source of fuel for the myth is that, in an important sense, we really don't *want* poverty to go away. It is therefore *convenient* to believe that the poor will always be with us (as they have always been). We don't want poverty to go away for at least two broad reasons.

The first is that our economic system necessarily generates poverty; but more specifically, our own employment increasingly depends on it. One day at Amos House, a young man was ejected from the soup kitchen for a rule infraction. On the curb outside, he shouted back at our social worker, "You know, if it wasn't for *me, you* wouldn't have a job!" I still ponder that remark ten years later.

Automation and cheap foreign labor have challenged our economy to find new ways to sustain growth and keep people busy and our economy has responded brilliantly. The service 'industry' has taken up the slack. As the Agricultural/Industrial Revolution displaced not only laborers, but also the life-sustaining role of small communities (tribes and then villages), it created tremendous neediness and marginalization, adding to the effects of automation. The demand for services to address mounting social problems provided the new raw material. Private and public service programs nicely fit the bill because they ease the pain and give the *appearance* of an effective response without actually solving the problem. Indeed, the kinds of short-term, palliative interventions provided by services often permit the problem to worsen long term. More material. Additionally, this neat economic solution has inspired the cultural fabrication of more frivolous needs and wants to which an infinite number of new services can be introduced to stoke the furnace.

A second reason why we cling to the continuation of poverty, and also to marginalization more broadly, is that many of us, at least, need a place to actively express our care and compassion. We need people — beyond our immediate family members — to care for in the absence of the tribal context within which we once freely shared our care with other members in a mutual support network. I'm like my dog, Pearl, who without the opportunity to hunt instinctively, finds herself having to play out the hunt in our house or backyard (sometimes in absurdly comical ways). I can't say that humans are instinctively compassionate or that we were *meant* by God or anything else to live in tribes. But there is clearly a compassionate streak in us, expressed more in some people than in others, and humans have lived tribally for ninety-nine percent of our time on earth. Tribalism is a way of life that has tested out, notwithstanding its relatively recent setback in the face of our own civilizational expansion. Despite how the balance of this competition appears to us, it is too early to call the match.

Mutual care, generated more by survival needs and self-interest than by altruism, is the basis of support in the tribe. In our world, this support has been supplanted by services, mainly professional services working within a service system. *Service, in fact, is simply the attempt to meet needs outside the context of community.* Just as we do not use the word 'service' to label the care we provide within our families, likewise there is no equivalent concept of 'service' among tribal people. For individuals with an especially caring disposition, the service system provides the only available outlet, other than the care provider's own family. The weakening nuclear family, however, like the extended family, clan, village and tribe before it, has increasingly surrendered its support function to professional services. Following this trend, we could *all* soon find ourselves supported by service providers alone.

John McKnight makes a compelling case that the professional service system is a poor substitute for the kind of support system only a genuine community can provide. It is inferior on many counts, not the least of which is that it frustrates the caring service provider who enters the field of teaching, health care or social work in order to give care only to face one systemic obstacle after another trying to do so. McKnight insists that the professional service system and its network of private and public institutions and agencies are not geared to providing care, only professional services. To give and receive care, there is no substitute for community. I consider the tribe to be the archetype of community in this sense.

So far I have identified our collectively held assumption that "the poor will always be with us" as a tragic, self-fulfilling prophecy based on mistaken assumptions. I have also named four factors contributing to the perpetuation of the myth and the consequent perpetuation of poverty:

1. We collectively believe that human poverty is an inevitable part of the natural order in general and of the nature of humans in particular.
2. We believe that, in fact, the poor have always been with us.
3. An increasing number of jobs and institutions (and the economy itself) depend on the continuation or worsening of poverty and marginalization.

4. The marginalized provide caregivers somewhere to direct their compassion.

A revised understanding of the inevitability of poverty lends itself to at least two general change strategies. Although activists like myself tend to favor more action-sounding suggestions, the first and perhaps most radical thing we can do is help surface our cultural mythology and replace it with principles of living that will work better for us — and possibly lead to the elimination of poverty. For "the poor will always be with us" we might substitute something like: The universe consists of cycles of creation and destruction, birth and death, but within this framework "the earth will provide." Our planet and its abundant and richly diverse community of life offer an adequate and acceptable support system for us, as it does for all other species. No one should languish in the kind of marginal destitution we commonly call 'poverty'. This strategy is one of learning and relearning.

The second avenue is building community — finding small and more ambitious ways of reintegrating ourselves into small-scale economies of support founded on trusting relationships. In *My Ishmael,* author Daniel Quinn distinguishes between a tribal economy founded on the exchange of human energy:

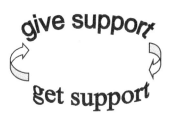

and our economy that is founded on the exchange of products, including service products:

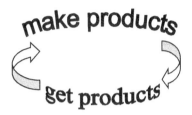

To the extent that we can transfer our faith and reliance from the product system to the communal support system we contribute to the atrophy (and eventual elimination) of the products system, its institutions and political structures and jurisdictions. The kind of poverty we are familiar with has been with us through the emergence of our civilization because it is *inherent* in the culture of our civilization, if not in civilization as a mode of social organization in general. Poverty can be eliminated, but it will require a fundamental break from the way we have been thinking and living.

Our current worldview, allegiances and psychological attachments strongly favor the prevailing way of life, as does the usual default assumption that the world is simply *going* to continue on its trajectory toward a more and bigger version of what we have today. But like a recessive gene, our capacity to trust the earth and live by each other's support and unique gifts lies within each of us, dormant for the most part, but ready to surface and engage after an initial adjustment process. Many disaffected youth, still partially dependent on the products system, have nevertheless chosen to live tribally

simply to support their refusal to eke out a living in the usual
way, preferring the freedom and vitality of life on the outside.
Less dramatic experiments, ranging from intentional rural
communities to urban block association activity, point in the
'give support/get support' direction.

By the standards of tribal wealth, even our financially well off
are quite poor. In my facilitation work with the materially
comfortable in churches and nonprofits, I find a surprising
receptivity to this disturbing message. A million dollars, for
example, is not enough to insure against having to spend the
last decade of life in a nursing home. One source of hope for
me — as distant as it appears — lies in the potential for defection within the middle and upper classes. As 'winning' the
products contest rewards us with a life that is increasingly
accelerated, virtual, alienating and superficial — as well as
ecologically perilous — the rewards of abandoning the game
we play for life with the trees and sky — and each other — will
prove increasingly irresistible. The simple living trend of the
past decade may portend a shift that is deeper and more widespread; this shift could provide a catalyst for the cultural break
necessary to end poverty.

It certainly lies outside the box to imagine rich people releas-
ing their hold on product wealth and the means of creating it,
but this will be a natural side effect of their shifting attention
in the direction of acquiring a different kind of wealth. The
marginalized poor would then have a better chance of reestab-
lishing access to land resources. Unfortunately, the prevailing
models of development in poor communities and countries
are the models offered by the products system, which the

poor themselves generally look to as the only way out. Alternatively, organizations committed to reducing poverty should emphasize strategies that regenerate the kind of self-reliant, give support/get support community life that can regenerate the kind of wealth we have paved over with a product-driven culture of winners and losers.

Then he replied, "consider the lilies of the field and the birds of the air..."

Out of Love[*]

"**I** *hate* love," Karla snapped, after Lin confessed his love for her in Gregory Roberts' autobiographical novel, *Shantaram*. Romantic love is reliable only to disappoint, to end badly. She couldn't trust it.

I'm beginning to share Karla's scarred cynicism, compelled to take a long look after the ending of my own twenty-year marriage a few years ago. I suspect there's more to this scenario than bad luck, sour grapes or just being a jerk. We loved each other and maybe still do, raised two children we both love and care for very much. We grew apart, became or discovered that we were incompatible partners, plagued by irreconcilable differences. We parted well and continue to relate and co-parent nicely together, apart.

I began my search for understanding with the observation that no one I know well receives the love they need. Not by a lot. And I can't dismissively conclude that it's just the people I know, or that 'it's always been this way,' or 'that's life'. The love is there, I believe, but the flow channels, both within and between us are often and largely clogged.

---

[*] A version of this essay first appeared in *The Fifth Estate*, Fifth Estate #394, Summer 2015.

In the long course of our culture's evolution, I venture, romantic love has now become the primary post-pubescent source of love in our world. But romantic love has not always occupied this special position. I concede the assumption that it is a universal in human experience, but in our globalized culture, romance has intensified over the millennia into a distorted caricature of versions common in tribal and Neolithic-type village societies.

We need love pretty much like we need food, and I think a useful parallel can be drawn between our source of food and our source of love. The pleasant tasting, sweet, salty and fatty foods have always controlled our eating patterns, but as Michael Pollan points out, the intensity of these food values is moderated in the natural diets of hunter-gatherers and simple agriculturalists. Our commercialized food industry has managed to winnow away all but the salt, the sugar and the fat, delivering a junk food diet. Way too many people are now consuming way too many food calories in the form of intensely sweet, salty and/or fatty food-like 'delicacies'. These commodities have become a substitute for real food. And the results, to say the least, are disappointing. Pleasures are superficial and fleeting; health is compromised.

Romantic love likewise offers an acutely intensified form of love, a 'delicacy' extracted from sources that are much less intense, but over time, more evenly satisfying. Two of these sources are what we might call 'community' and 'nature', inadequate labels meaning, very roughly: a) a small group of trustworthy individuals/families whose interdependent, face-to-face personal support is the basis of their survival;

and b) the features of the group's local environment that are not man-made. Our 'love diet' no longer recognizes these very bland-seeming sources of love, but if we really want to feel held, safe, loved, there may be no substitute.

There's a relevant scene in the documentary, *God Grew Tired of Us*, in which four refugees among the Sudanese 'lost boys' are sitting in their new Pittsburgh apartment lamenting the loss of all they left behind in the Kenyan refugee camp (and, by extension, in the Sudanese village life they faintly recall). "There's just the four of us [here together]...that's not enough," one of the young men explains. Four, in more words, is not enough to generate and sustain the love, care and support he needs. Not in the least a dismissal of his three roommates, or a reference to the absence of women in their unit, the comment is a simple observation that the young man needs an entire *community* to support him. Reflecting on our nuclear families and binary love relationships, it's clear that *two* is not enough. Two is *not* enough. We are constantly being told, mostly indirectly, that two *is* sufficient, that two *should* be sufficient, that one or both of you are the problem if the two of you are not working out to *be* sufficient.

For humans, we should be learning by now, two doesn't work. To claim that people were *meant* to live in tribe-like communities or that community living can't be brutal and ugly is neither useful nor, I believe, truthful. It is also the case that marriage (mono- and polygamous, hetero- and homosexual, serial and life-lasting) and household units have been common features of tribal and small village life. But the basic form of social organization of the tribe and small village, within which marital households are sustained, is a form that worked for people, to get the love as well as the food they required, over the course of human evolution and has prevailed as the way of life for ninety-nine percent of that history. Community life works for people in the same way that flock life has worked for geese and pack life works for wolves. As a very basic form, it does not provide good living, but it provides a basis — a necessary condition — for good living, including getting the love we need, delivered in the form of care and devotion, sustained and reliable.

At least two particular features of traditional tribal and village life that are not inherent in community living defined more broadly are noteworthy as powerful sources of love in these communities. The first is culture, which guides the thinking and behavior of people living in traditional communities. It also provides meaning. The guidance and meaning culture provides constitute an indirect source of love, a security blanket for its members growing into its world. The modern, especially urban child is exposed to cultural variety, but also cultural confusion and contention. We are lost and anxious in the stew of the mixed messages we receive from the Big (global, nontraditional) Culture and the remnants of its assimilated subcultures.

The second feature common among traditional societies is an infant care practice that essentially inoculates children with a starter dose of love in the first months of life. Slipped from the womb directly into the warm hands of community members, newborns are virtually never let go by these hands and warm bodies until they push away several months later, ready for the independence of crawling and toddling. The initial 'in-arms' phase is associated with on-demand breastfeeding, which continues through the child's first few years, again, until the child stops coming around altogether. The love (and knowledge) stored up in these early months and years makes for an older child and adult who is confident and secure, loved and secure in love.

The love we derive from the land, directly and indirectly through the network of community relationships, is less obvious, but only because it is obscured by the profound alienation from the earth that has accompanied life in the modern world. A serious consequence of this alienation has been a silent, but deeply profound loss of reverence and gratitude. We cannot give thanks for gifts we can't see or recognize. We all know what 'Mother Earth' means on some level. The sun and the earth, very especially the small patch of the earth that traditionally each tribe and village intimately knew, worshipped and relied on for survival, are the ultimate sources of love, of care and devotion. They provide and keep providing, from cradle to grave. Studies have shown that people are just a little happier simply to have some trees to gaze at through their apartment building windows. 'Love' might not be the first word from the lips of modern gardeners, hunters, fishers and ranchers when asked to identify what they get from their work activity, but that's basically what it is, or part of what it is.

There are media-celebrated instances of 'happy-ever-after' love relationships in our world. I believe in these relationships, and know couples who appear to be creating and sharing a lasting partnership in love. There is also a lot of 'quiet desperation' among us, couples holding it together, without the love they need. But I think there's another parallel here, this one between romantic love and the 'American Dream'. The myth of the 'American Dream' is that any poor person can climb the ladder of success and become financially comfortable, maybe rich. A few make it, everyone knows. The system insures that the percentage who make it is very low. The implication that *every* poor person can succeed is the lie we swallow in the myth. Happy, long-lasting marriages built on falling-in-love platforms are no doubt happening still. But the number of happy endings is noticeably dipping from very few to even fewer, in step with the fraying of community and our ties to the earth, not coincidentally. The myth of romantic love, like the 'American Dream', continues to be delivered with enough cultural packaging to keep enough of us believing that it will give us the love we need. It seldom does.

Romantic attraction, to the extent that it is an embellishment of sexual attraction, is probably universal in human experience, if only for the obvious purpose it serves to keep the experience going. But why, in the course of our civilization's development, have we placed this useful, feel-good attraction on steroids? I speculate that romantic love has become overblown in order to reinforce a host of other forces in our culture that pry the individual from the community. On the one hand, the operating system of our culture compels it to absorb the many diverse cultures of the world into itself, to unify. 'Globalization' sometimes refers to this. On the other, within its globalizing mass, the culture relentlessly separates its members from each other (starting at birth!) and fragments much of our lives, what we think and what we do. Romantic love has achieved exaggerated prominence as a cultural tool to isolate pairs from the group. It reinforces the 'rugged individualism' of our culture. Bad endings in love are culturally supported for the same purpose — the isolated pair becomes two isolated individuals. The economy of our culture feasts on love-needy, community-less individuals. Consumerism is largely rooted in the loss of love, in particular, and more generally, on the loss of the personal and material support provided by communities and land bases.

In this era of failing love, people are resorting to a variety of ways to fill the void beyond attempts at romantic relationships. Sex, very noticeably, has been distilled from love of any sort. Eating sugar right out of the bowl. Addiction and compulsion in general, so widespread and intense in our society, may be functions of love lost, at least in part. And there are the countless, more subtle ways we compensate. There is a 'rebound' quality to all of our love affairs, as well as to the various substitutes. With every romantic attraction, fulfilled and unfulfilled, we are rebounding from a break-up, from our broken relationship with the caregivers of the community and the natural environment that for most of us have grown distant well beyond memory.

Without the love we need, we hurt. We hurt others, we internalize the hurt and hurt ourselves. We're becoming a society of junkies, in the grip of cultural forces, collective patterns of thinking and acting that we did not design or ever consciously endorse. We sustain these forces, however, through the unconscious sponsorship of our minds, every day.

And then through our choices and the patterns of our collective behavior, every day. Short on love, long on addiction, violence, domination. Love does not pass easily in our world.

At the very least and short of any measures we might take to rework our world, we can and must unblock the pathways of love, both within ourselves — to love ourselves — and between ourselves and others, as best we can. At the individual level, the struggle to love and be loved should not be abandoned as we begin to grasp how little we get from our efforts. Falling and being in love are uniquely beautiful experiences, I cannot and need not deny. Something so irresistible has nonetheless become so full of disappointment. I have so often heard, and as many times conceded, that failed love is more a consequence of excessive expectations than of conflict or loss of interest. At a powerfully emotional level, we unconsciously expect our lover to fill us with all the love we have over the decades and centuries forfeited by living the way we now collectively do. Plumbing the depths of this disconnect between expectation and outcome can surely help us adjust the former, and our perspective more generally, as we proceed in relationship and partnership building.

Like Karla, and so many others, I have been tempted to avoid love altogether and tough it out. Alternatively, I can embrace love and avoid — or change — our culture. Rework our world. But like any other recovery challenge, this alternative is daunting and demanding. It is a collective more than an individual recovery challenge. It entails a substantial con-spiracy (literally, a 'breathing together') to renounce with others the mythologies of our culture, to begin or continue to re-form small communities, and to reacquaint ourselves with the sustaining earth and sky around us. Into this wider and deeper basket of care, the love that lovers enjoy will settle, if we follow the longer way there.

Saint Dorothy[*]

Dorothy Day was a large part of why I first showed up twenty-three years ago to work at Amos House, Providence's Catholic Worker-inspired house of hospitality. Following four years as an irregular volunteer I moved in to the house and joined the 'staff'; three years later I became the 'director'. Soon after this transition I discovered that a scattering of people here and there were calling me a 'saint'. Maybe it had something to do with my privileged upbringing that I seemed to be renouncing, or perhaps it was my choice to work with 'the poor' instead of some other needy population. Maybe it was the meager Catholic Worker compensation I received. Although I left Amos House five years ago and clearly sense that my reputation as a saint, or fool (or saintly fool), hasn't followed me very closely, I am challenged to consider the meaning and ramifications of the now official campaign to canonize Dorothy Day, my formative inspiration.

Dorothy herself was consistently and genuinely hostile to any association of her with sainthood and her hostility expressed a general aversion to the concept beyond its official or unofficial application in her case. Clearly she bristled at the 'S' word *not*

---

[*] This essay first appeared as "Change in Culture is What's Needed, as Dorothy Day Knew" in the *National Catholic Reporter*, February 16, 2001.

from the perspective that she was unworthy of the label, if ever she had an opinion on this matter one way or another. I won't raise an objection if the Catholic Church chooses to declare her saintliness, but as an occasionally faithful follower of Dorothy's, I'm moved by her spirit to extend and embellish her case for distrusting sainthood itself.

Dorothy insisted that the label amounted to a dismissal of the meaning of her life and words. In this sense, sainthood is a defense against the truth. When she becomes a 'saint', the rest of us become instantly exempt from the call of her teachings and witness. The act of canonization displaces responsibility. Perhaps this implies that deification lets us off the hook in a similar way. We can reasonably be expected to follow another man or woman, but surely not a saint, much less a god.

A bit deeper into the role of the saint in our culture, I find that sainthood also defends against the truth by promoting an individualistic worldview. The conflicting messages of saint-hood are:

a) the examples of saintly lives can be dismissed because they're lived by unusually graced individuals, and
b) the nasty world we live in *can* be transcended, as exemplified by these individual heroes.

Though contradictory, both messages subtly enable and support the oppressive status quo, with version (b) resembling the more secular Horatio Alger myth. I think it's very common for people to subscribe to both messages at once: "Because there are people (the saints) who made the grade,

I'm accountable for my own failure, but since the saints are so extraordinary they've earned their own special label, there's no way I can be expected to be so holy." Like the burgeoning focus on celebrity in our culture, sainthood fixation promotes the cheerleading spectator rather than the active participant and at the same time calms any worry that there is a systemic source of our social and spiritual ailments.

For those more committed to social transformation, sainthood takes on a different, but no less individualistic, interpretation: "If only (some critical mass of) people followed the example of Saint _____, the world would be the place we want it to be." The way to improve the world is to get people to be better than they are. Intending to move society from the status quo, this understanding of sainthood has the opposite effect by promoting the moral behavior of the *individual* rather than the *systemic* basis of our social problems. Our culture, by which I mean the global culture of civilization, and its supporting mythology, are what fuel the social distress in our society. It was partly in response to the mounting level of this distress that our modern religions historically emerged in the first place. Neither the world's troubled condition, nor its salvation, is a matter of how good, bad or saintly are the thoughts and behavior of individual people. It is much more a function of how we think and live *collectively*. The problems (and solutions) associated with motor vehicles, for example, lie in the cultural flow that compels most everyone to drive (or want to drive), not in a moral or other character deficiency we could identify in each of the drivers. With the exception of a saintly individual here and there, people aren't going to *get* any better than they are. No amount of pleading and whipping is going to snap ordinary people out of the habit of following the flow. This is true of people in our culture and any other.

Peter Maurin, Dorothy's founding partner in the Catholic Worker initiative, insisted that we must create a society in which it is "easy to be good." Perhaps it is an unintended application of this wonderful thought to suggest that instead of laboring to make ourselves and others into saints, we should help transform our culture so that *average* people will be compelled by the cultural flow to share, yield and cooperate in community living, respect the earth and celebrate in the simple joys of living. We contribute to this transformation by exposing and recanting the mythology that undergirds our culture and by experimenting with new ways of living. The culture will change one person at a time, but the goal is a new worldview and social habits that are held *collectively* by ordinary people bearing the usual variety of personal gifts and shortcomings.

A final dimension of our sainthood fascination can be illuminated by the absence of saint, prophet, savior, guru or avatar concepts (as *we* know them) in nature-based, tribal cultures that have survived in relative isolation from us for thousands of years. Presumably these cultures have never found a *need* for sainthood and the like. I can't imagine that tribal cultures such as the Yequana Indians of the Amazon would assume that there's some depraved human condition that calls for redemption or transcendence. In the context of our very different culture, attempting what saintly people like Dorothy Day attempt can be understood as an effort to survive in a profoundly dysfunctional society without going crazy. Daniel

Berrigan has defended his acts of civil disobedience by insisting that he is merely protecting his soul from being captured by the machine. While many of us seem to prosper in our troubled society, many try desperately to make sense of the world by 'acting out' in one of a variety of ways. In this sense, the 'saint' response is not so much a rising above the rest, but a kind of coping mechanism; it is one defense strategy against a culture gone mad. Functional, sustainable cultures would not — and ordinarily do not — produce saints. Contrary to the 'noble savage' perception many people have of, say, Australia's aboriginal people, you won't find a saint (as we might recognize one) among them, only ordinary people with the usual individual idiosyncrasies living in the flow of a culture that works.

This cultural comparison suggests that we quit falling over ourselves to recognize and adore the lotus rising out of the muck and instead concentrate on the muck. So long as we choose to live in muck, a lotus will surely rise now and again — and twelve year-old boys will come to school and spray real bullets at their schoolmates. We can get at the muck by recognizing that it grows from and is shaped by our culture, regardless of how virtuous or vicious are any one of our individual members relative to the others. The culture has, as it were, a life of its own, and a strong will to sustain itself. Its baseline sustenance is its mythology, which we collectively live out every day and accept as fact, without a thought given to it. The 'facts' provided by this mythology, explaining who we are and how things came to be the way they are, apply only to one culture, our own, though we mistake them for explaining the human story in its entirety. Shifting our attention from transcendence to the struggle of more ordinary people to survive the system, we can transform the culture that has us *all* transfixed. With a revised understanding of who we are, where we've come from and where we're heading, we will create both a new cultural mythology and new way of living on the earth and with each other.

Like Clare and Francis of Assisi, Lao Tzu and some of the others we might call 'saints', Dorothy Day certainly challenged our culture in this radical manner as she also transcended it. And as I continue my own personal efforts to become a more mindful, compassionate and nonviolent presence in my home and in the world, I am not at all critical of choosing a way of life as an individual that others may want to consider 'saintly'. I also depend for guidance and inspiration on the examples of many whom others might call 'saints'. I urge only a shift in perspective on what this means.

Since leaving Amos House, my own ministry has shifted, as my understanding has shifted. Though I continue to support worthy programs, campaigns and movements of the kind I contributed to for many years, I have become more committed to learning and teaching about our collective need to untie our cultural shackles and the process of how this might unfold. Raising these questions and experimenting with living alternatives using the tools available to me, I hope to contribute to a change in the flow of our society that promises something better.

School Reform:
A Systems View

Communities across the country are frustrated with their schools and school systems. Teachers, administrators, parents, unions, legislators and, of course, the children, are variously blamed, and also frustrated. Systems thinking, which starts by recognizing the influence of systemic behavior in contrast to the direct impact of individuals and institutions, is a perceptual tool that can help relieve some of this frustration.

A systems thinker might ask, in response to school frustration, "What purpose might our schools be serving effectively if they are not effectively serving the purpose we want and intend for them to serve?" Also, "Recognizing that systems are never 'closed', but must interface with other systems, with what systems are schools required to interface that might illuminate the source of frustration?"

Over time, systems interact, they self-organize, to the point where they become nested inside each other. For example, our bodies are systems — a collection of parts working together in a relatively coherent manner to achieve a purpose (survival and health, without getting too detailed or philosophical). The respiratory system is 'nested' within the whole body system. Not aware of the broader purpose, the respiratory system normally plays its part faithfully in meeting the needs of the whole body system.

Human rationality and volition notwithstanding, our more contrived social systems behave in a similarly predictable manner. Our school systems, as an example, are nested within the wider economic system, now global is reach, and therefore must contribute to its purpose. Schools do not seem to nest perfectly within our economy — businesses often complain that school graduates are not sufficiently skilled (in technical areas mostly) and that too many kids drop out.[*] It should, however, provide some relief to recognize and affirm some of the more basic if unheralded ways our school system does a respectable job of serving the wider economic system. Three are particularly relevant:

A. The school system (as a national and increasingly global totality) regulates the flow of young people into the workforce. One way to see how this systemic interaction works is to notice the rough correlation between the increasing number of grade levels children have been required by law to pass through over the past one hundred and fifty years and the improvement of pro-

---

[*] This frustration might itself find relief upon viewing the wider systemic picture. While we freely recognize a globalized economy, we assess school systems locally (district, city, state, nation), but not beyond that point. Schooling worldwide, as a systemic, self-organized whole, is struggling to serve the global economy, to keep up and adapt. If we can judge how schools are managing this globally, we will appreciate how well they are in fact performing.

duction technology that has permitted more work to get done with fewer workers. Students must continue to *consume,* but must be kept on the production sidelines until needed. School is the way we keep children occupied while the adults work.

B. Related to this function, schools do a decent job of *sifting* this workforce flow, ensuring that young people fill the needed spots in the workforce, at the right levels. This function is more deliberately executed by many school systems abroad, whereas in the States there lingers a self-defeating ideal that everyone can and should earn a college degree. The fantasy of equal opportunity and job placements for all who graduate in the U.S. does little to prevent the school system from serving its economic sifting function.

C. Aside from the thorny development that many young Americans over the decades have apparently lost enthusiasm for the success program offered by our culture, schools have played their part pretty well in conditioning them to be good workers. If the primary systemic purpose of schools is to regulate and sift the flow of youth into the workforce, their secondary purpose is to prepare them for it. The emphasis for this preparation is workplace *behavior* — working for the external reward of money and promotion (replacing grades, credits), obeying and pleasing the boss (teacher), feeling comfortable or used to sitting and working in regimented factory or office stations (desks in rows), living with hierarchy and arbitrariness, ugly spaces, etc. Children are to students, Derrick Jensen laments, what cod are to fish sticks. *Less* emphasis is needed on acquiring specific job-related knowledge, the curricular content of schools, since the economic system features a 'work your way up' platform, and knowing too much upon entering actually *undermines* this arrangement. Perverse as it sounds, schools do all right in ensuring that all those hours of teaching do not translate into too much learning. We're supposed to "learn on the job."

A systems 'trap' (or 'tragedy') develops when systems created by public policy and/or self-organization produce results that all the individual players, making their individual contributions, work hard to generate but do not, in the end, want or like. I can't imagine that Horace Mann and other social reformers who successfully lobbied for compulsory schooling back in the mid-nineteenth century recognized that their liberal intentions related to helping young people from all classes learn and mature were essentially a systemic ploy by the economy to keep children from underfoot. It *was* part of Mann's design, however, to use schooling to discipline youth for employment as an important dimension of their learning.[*] Beyond this training, personal growth and genuine learning do occur to various degrees in schools, as they surely did for me, but schools are not structured *principally* to do this. And there are, I believe, better tools for this.

---

[*] Horace Mann, Twelfth Annual Report as Secretary of Massachusetts State Board of Education, 1848.

The beauty, power and danger of systems under momentum lie in the ability and tendency of systems to create their own behavior, as if they have a volitional mind of their own. None of us who suffer from the intransigence of failing schools are victims of conspiracy. Systems self-organize like a tornado, and in the process coordinate with neighboring systems to reinforce each other. This is especially true of subsystems, systems that must nest themselves within wider systems.

Our global monoculture is itself a system — a collection of parts (sometimes called 'memes') that interact to create and sustain a relatively coherent whole. The purpose of culture is to show us how to live and give our lives meaning. Our global economic system is a creation of our culture and nests within it. And so it must be here, with culture, and its narrative — our collective story, our paradigm, our worldview — that marks our entry point to social transformation deep enough to break us out of our schooling rut. Short of the real utility of lowering our expectations of what schools do and can do, there's little relief from schools that disappoint without changing the economy, which largely hinges on changing the culture. There's no end-around or pass-through. Same culture, same thinking, same everything else, essentially. Yet while culture presents itself as much an unmovable object as it is a powerful leverage point for change, its grip extends no further nor deeper than in the sponsorship of our unreflective minds.

Space here permits but a simple suggestion for one place to begin this cultural shift — a close look at how poorly the system of our culture and its subsystems (starting with our global economy) are nesting within the system of the earth, our collective home. The planetary system is non-negotiable. It is becoming increasingly clear that human survival here requires a fundamental adjustment in how we live in it.

With some large measure of humility, we must consult with earth's systems and restructure our own to fit. I believe this adjustment will lead quickly to others. Education isn't going away as we make this transition, but I strain to see schools as we know them at the other end. In the meantime, all of us working in or otherwise connected with schools can take the step by adjusting our expectations.

Secret Lessons of
Francis of Assisi[*]

Around the age of eighteen, I found inspiration in the life and teachings of Jesus, but soon after I was awoken even more intensely by the particular discipleship of Francis of Assisi. Many know this attraction. For me, the life and legend of Francis spoke to a desire for simplicity in a world of addictive consumerism, nonviolence in a time of unprecedented killing, courageous resistance in the face of blind conformity and a direct sort of spirituality in place of shallow and compartmentalized rituals. Though my Franciscan inspiration has sustained itself over the three intervening decades, I have recently discovered that my appreciation has been renewed by my exposure to five lessons Francis failed to get across to me in my youth, in spite of my adoration. Perhaps these are lessons he shared very clearly in his life and words, and I'm sure I nodded faithfully to most of them, but evidently I was not prepared to receive them until other influences opened my mind and arms to them years later.

Francis linked the meaning of his own life with the natural world and its beautiful, abundant and diverse community of life. He interpreted Christ's message as earth-centered and

---

[*] A version of this essay first appeared in *Sacred Journey*, December 2003.

conditioned his personal fulfillment on his ability to reimmerse himself in this community. People around him, and throughout the civilized world, fancied themselves somehow apart from and above other life forms. At twenty, I regarded Francis' tree hugging quaint and noble, but found the popular culture's emphasis on this devotion of his a bit annoying. Now I understand the paradigm shift he must have experienced. Our use of the word 'nature' is but one reflection of our collective misunderstanding that *we* are something *else*. With this mindset, we have waged war against other life as if the earth were ours alone, presuming that humans are exempt from the limits imposed on other life forms in their quest to survive and expand. Calling the birds and hounds 'brothers' and 'sisters', Francis expressed the understanding that we are *part* of the earth and its community of life. Lesson number one.

Subsequent to his defection from Assisi and the prevailing social order, Francis found a second source of meaning beyond his new discipleship and fresh sense of belonging to the earth's community of life. Followers of his inspiring example formed a community of *people* who supported one another on all levels. Thinking only in terms of how Francis and Clare as *individuals* lived so differently from those they left behind, I never considered their many Assisian followers as anything more than followers, inspired as I had been inspired. But the forming of the egalitarian community itself was a dramatic departure from the highly stratified, commercialized and oppressive social and economic order Francis and his followers had known before. Lesson number two.

Francis' repudiation of books (other than the Scriptures) I completely dismissed as simply rash and unappreciative of the different ways different people learn and explore. Books have always figured prominently in my learning and personal growth process. Lately, though, I'm beginning to see what might have been the source of his stubbornness. Today, we place an unquestioning premium on literacy and perceive literacy training as a vehicle for social mobility, but fail to recognize that the written word has always been both a source and product of social inequality. Secondly, while all cultural symbols serve to mediate in one way or another our experience of reality, literacy created a whole new order of mediation. For the blessings of literacy we have nevertheless traded a manner of living and experiencing reality that is more direct and immediate. This tradeoff has hardened off over time some of our sensory and extrasensory capacities, leaving us partially numb to the world around us. A third lesson.

In departing from Assisi the way he did, Francis was also defecting from society and its culture. This is a very different way of looking at this momentous transition than how I perceived it initially. I didn't *see* culture. I didn't see that in abandoning the conventional life of Assisi he was also abandoning civilization itself, or at least the culture of *his* civilization. He brought his Bible, yes, and he held on to the Church (what if the Pope had later denied him?), but left his sword, his money as well as the prevailing models of individualism, competition, acquisitiveness, domination, social stratification and redemptive violence. He walked away culturally as well as physically (though not completely in either respect) and tried to live a different way altogether. If there was any doubt that his intention was cultural defection and not simply running away from home, surely this matter was clarified when Francis spoiled the sacred taboo — the culturally universal taboo — against public nudity and dropped his clothing off before heading out. Lesson four.

Years ago I largely ignored the manner in which Francis framed his conversion as it was presented to me. What was at the bottom of his departure? He was suddenly ignited by a new understanding of Christ and his message, a message that spoke fundamentally to his simple desire for human happiness and a kind of freedom that confers this happiness. I had a different notion of what saintliness was about and it had more to do with self-sacrifice and altruism. At most, personal happiness was a byproduct of a more other-regarding mission. By my way of thinking, saving the world was a matter of getting people to be more saintly, like Francis, to rise above their self-interest and care about suffering and degradation here and afar and act on this passion. I still encourage this kind of consciousness raising, but I also understand that if ordinary people could have ready access to the sources of what will make them genuinely free, happy and fulfilled, we would all get to the promised land a lot more quickly, and arrive there *together*. There's a few standing in line for sainthood; everybody's in line to enjoy life. Lesson number five.

Having missed these important lessons, I sometimes wonder what I *did* learn from my early exposure to Francis. At the same time, my current interpretations of these lessons and how I associate them with Francis are no doubt shaped by other influences as much as by the facts of the man's life themselves. But learning these lessons over the past few years has affected how I perceive and relate to the natural world, of which I see more clearly that I am a part. One small expression of this shift is that I have moved my morning prayer and meditation practice from sitting inside to walking through a nearby city park. I have applied the lesson of community by emphasizing in my teaching and workshop facilitation the need to regenerate community bonds, but I've also become acquainted with nearly all thirty-eight families living on my block in Providence. Nearly every block household participated in a recently completed 'consultation exchange' directory that provides a way for neighbors to lend each other their expertise and help solve problems. I have come a long way in shedding, on the one hand, my prejudice against wisdom and intelligence that isn't tied to formal schooling and book learning, and on the other (and with a degree of irony), my obsession with saintliness. For years I wanted to be like Francis and tried hard to live out this calling. Voluntary poverty, celibacy, homeless shelter and soup kitchen life were my devotions. I'm trying much harder now to appreciate the humble calling to be happy and, well, ordinary, to share with everyone else this simple desire without having to rise above spiritually and morally. As extraordinary as Francis was, his genuine identification with the guy in the crowd is the gift I am left holding.

Most dramatically, though, my reacquaintance with Francis has compelled me to believe that these 'new' lessons speak forcefully to the current human predicament and not just to my spiritual journey as an individual seeker. The world's civilized human population continues to surge toward its own extinction at a frightening pace as it depletes available resources and despoils its natural habitat. And at the same exponential rate we continue to tear the remnant bonds of community life, creating a world of isolated individuals struggling to compete for survival, recognition and fortune in an anonymous global marketplace. Francis' choice to defect has become a live option for me, but not for me as an individual, rather for me with others, hundreds and thousands and millions of others. I have lost faith in efforts to address social problems with the tools provided within the social systems that currently support us. Our civilization, driven and formed by an inherently dysfunctional culture, is a sinking Titanic. Yet it is merely a more evolved version of the same civilization and culture that Francis chose to abandon eight hundred years ago. My recent vocational direction has centered on promoting a dialogue around this question: What would it mean for us to make a fresh start, together?

Ordinary people with ordinary wants and dreams, gifts and shortcomings, inside the Christian faith and out, can and will respond to the suggestion that our joy and delight in life are tied up with our connection to the earth and to each other, in small circles of equals, offering our special gifts and receiving unconditional support. In my dialogue facilitation work I am consistently discovering a very wide receptivity to what is the most radical proposal I have ever seriously entertained: starting over fresh instead of continuing to tinker with the system. Affluent and poor, liberal and conservative, people engage in the dialogue as an uplifting departure from the usual remedies that keep us plodding along. It will become apparent, I believe, to more and more of us that living free and satisfying lives together will mean walking away, somewhat like Francis did, from the dominant systems we so depend on now and experimenting in new directions. Our collective survival, not just personal holiness, is on the line.

Memoirs of the Oldest
(and Guiltiest) Man

As a kid I belonged to one of the Caucasian tribes we called the Akarum (that's at least how I would try to spell it now), living near the Tigris River. I can vividly recall, though it's been roughly eleven thousand two hundred and nine or ten years, my uncle Noab speaking with my dad over improving our band's planting ritual. The bands that planted back then seemed content just to stuff some seeds or branches from their favorite plants into the ground surrounding their sleeping shelters. My uncle, though, proposed that we try digging up and turning over a patch of ground and plant our seeds in a soil environment we could keep free of competitors, animal and vegetable. The seeds were taken mostly from the sweet grasses native to our area.

Between good luck and some prudent choices, I've managed to hang on long enough to witness just how profound and extensive the ripple effects of this conversation have been. The seeds my dad and his brother proceeded to sow that spring turned out to be the seeds of our civilization, of its gradual rise and expansion as well as the comparatively rapid decline and demise I'm observing outside my window today, in the early years of the 21st century.

My memory of subsequent events gets a bit fuzzy, but I know my Uncle's innovation eventually found favor among the other Akarum bands and over a number of generations our families reached the point where we no longer had to move to keep ourselves fed. All the while we also found ourselves hunting less. The intensive gardening style that evolved from my uncle's idea permitted a desirably settled way of life, but also required all of the tribal bands to live together. This changed how we interacted quite a bit. Because the change was so gradual, though, we adjusted. It seems like a blink-of-an-eye, but it must have taken many more generations before neighboring tribes found themselves blending into our village life. Our 'no competitors allowed' farming method had become more and more intense and aggressive because most advances in cultivation were rewarded with more and more food production. The food abundance attracted other tribes and anyhow we needed more territory to cultivate more food to feed our growing numbers.

In some ways life was clearly more satisfying in our 'consolidated' villages. We didn't have to pick up and move every year and most of the year food was easily accessible. Storage and irrigation replaced hunting and foraging as our primary survival challenges. We gave up some things, too, some we noticed at the time and others that came to light later on. The concept of 'work' — as a separate kind of activity — introduced itself into our consolidated culture. And work we did. Also, in spite of our clever way of collecting water and diverting it from the river, the weather occasionally spoiled our crops.

Later on they would call this 'famine', but there were years when many people died from crop failure.

*****

A number of connected drawbacks we are only now coming to appreciate stem from the impulse to expand territory for more cultivation and the social power generated by all the (good year) food surpluses. We kept having to expand and secure our borders to feed our people who were growing in numbers because of all the food we harvested. This created a new kind of conflict with neighboring tribes, which were forced to one degree or another to abandon both their tribal culture and their hunter-gatherer way of feeding themselves. (As we were developing our 'no competitor' farming alternative to foraging, other tribes to the south had caught on to herding domesticated animals instead of just hunting what may be around.) The consolidated culture had the effect of all but obliterating tribal distinctions and all that goes along with cultural differences. Among many other challenges this presented, our expanding villages had to devise some rules and order-keeping structures to compensate for the loss of individual tribal norms. Our villages grew into towns and towns merged into cities (mind you, this all took place over thousands of years, as far as I can recall). It got a little hectic.

Due to the social power stored in the silos, the rules and control structures devised by the people who held the silo keys heavily rewarded those people, who began to surround themselves with all kinds of riches and well-armed guardians paid to keep order in the city and expand its frontier as needed.

At this point — maybe halfway back (or five thousand years ago), a small empire began to form outward from the largest population center. The power base was in the food production system that dug up the earth, moved water around and kept any plant or animal that challenged crop growth out of crop's way, usually by killing them. But as the empire formed, the food power pumped itself into the increasingly large police and army forces and their increasingly sophisticated weaponry.

Even at this stage of the consolidated culture's evolution, I can't recall many people seriously doubting how good life was getting. I'm still referring to social changes that formed over generations, but by the time this way of life of ours started to move out of the general area, my people of the consolidated culture had begun to write some cultural mythology for itself that must have made my dad and uncle turn in their graves. At the time, though, none of us were aware of these gradual shifts and what they could mean down the line. Describing it in retrospect, I have to say that our people seemed to have adopted violence as an object of worship. The Babylonian gods, as they were later called, sanctified the regular exercise of violent power to crush evil, however interpreted. You see this religion still scripted today in most of our movies and cartoon shows. There's a good force and an evil one, well equipped to harm. After a predictable struggle — always of a violent nature — the force of good prevails by means of superior violence. It is the violence, ultimately, that redeems in the end and saves the day. The violent redeemer is usually a male, though that is changing.

Back in the tribal days, people got hurt and even killed by each other's hands and there was inter-tribal fighting of sorts here and there, but the order of violence worship that emerged in our culture really meant a whole new ball game. And as the consolidated culture moved outward to till more ground and expand the empire, tribal people in the way had to play this violent game or get completely squashed. Many tribes were exterminated — every member killed — but the least the others suffered was the decimation of their culture and way of life.

This is because another bit of mythology, something I can only describe as a kind of master race mentality, seeped into our culture to accompany the glorified violence. It's not as if individual people actually believed that humans were of some order distinct and superior to other life forms or that their particular race of humans was meant to rule all other people because only their race knew how people were meant to live (though many individuals have believed these things). But looking back at how we carried ourselves as a people, collectively, it seems obvious that this anthropocentrism and racism was a central part of our culture's operating mythology. People rule the planet, which was created essentially for us, and we rule the (other) people.

Though the center of imperial power shifted around through the generations, each empire more or less adopted and passed on this patterned cultural mythology as the consolidated culture spread out from our original area in all directions. Our culture's mode of organizing people was hierarchical in exaggerated proportions. I'm not talking about a chief or an elder with some leadership distinction, I mean one guy at the top of a big pyramid with tons of power and riches (they sometimes literally buried the riches with their dead bodies), a few associates around him on down to a bottom teeming with masses of slaves, serfs, soldiers, workers and then lots of others excluded from the zero-sum economic competition altogether.

As far as I can reach back, rich white men have been on top calling the shots right through the millennia. The men ruled over the women, and after the initial tribal assimilations, the tribal people we encountered in our global expansion were nearly all of them of darker skin. As my families traveled westward with the consolidated culture, the expansion seemed, in hindsight, quite slow in the beginning, but it sure did quicken these past few hundred years. We came to this American continent and discovered tribal people we called 'Indians'. Of course at the time there were thousands of distinct cultures of these people, but since we had long ago obliterated the cultural differences that so clearly demarcated one tribe from another (like when I was a boy), we just took them as a bunch of Indians, half-human savages really. As before, we most naturally gave them the choice of slavery (or some other demeaning form of assimilation) or death. We did the same thing in Africa with the tribal people there. It was a favor we thought we were performing. Make them Christians (our culture's flagship religion), give them a real life. We had as much pity on these folks as we did contempt for their barbaric lifestyles. In the consolidated culture, subcultural differences ceased to matter very much, but skin color continued to rule as a way to lock people into their appropriate position in the pyramid. People of color were stone-draggers.

"Women," as Yoko Ono declared, were the "niggers of the world" and poor people in general were simply poor because they deserved or were destined to be.

It was as if, using a sports analogy, the rich white men navigating the cultural steamroller believed that playing baseball was the only proper way for humans to make a living and insisted that everyone else, including tribal people who always got along playing various noncompetitive games, had to get with the baseball program. But since the women and people of color were considered inferior in all relevant respects, they were confined to field maintenance and bat boy jobs. It's difficult to exaggerate just how different the way tribal people made a living and organized themselves was from the money/commodification system (anchored in 'no-competitors' farming) that developed as the core of the consolidated culture. Not to mention vast differences in mythology, customs, religion, worldview, etc.

Due to the brutality of the genocidal assimilation process, the consolidated culture began to soften in places, establishing concepts of justice, rights and other protections. This has been mostly a defense mechanism to ensure that the program moves forward. With tremendous handicaps, including the powerful remnants of assimilation trauma, women and people of color have recently been permitted to compete on the field as players. Privileged white men continued to start off heavily advantaged. In limited ways, some nations of the consolidated culture occasionally offered 'new deals' to their marginalized populations, and every so often a country changed dealers, but everywhere it's basically the same game: make the economy bigger, consume the earth to feed and otherwise accommodate a growing population, push consumerism and do it through competitive, hierarchical structures and institutions. An observer from another planet would surely conclude that the overarching purpose of the culture and its systems is to enrich and empower the rich and the powerful. The observer might notice that the combined wealth of our world's approximately eight hundred billionaires today (we lost about three hundred in the crash of '08) is equal to the combined wealth of the poorest fifty percent of the entire population, roughly 3.4 billion humans. One billion people go to bed hungry most nights.

Virtually every institution within the consolidated culture fits the same template — they are hierarchical in relation to power, status and economic rewards and they are commodified at the core. Like our culture's codified laws, policies and propaganda, the culture's institutions, from the UN down to the soup kitchen, public and private, for profit and nonprofit, are vehicles through which the culture controls its six and a half billion people on its terms.

The school, for example, is a relatively recent innovation necessitated by the rapid growth in the number of people needed to be controlled. Schools provided a way to separate children from the working community of adults where they became increasingly dispensable due to automation. Schools also trained children to conform to the competitive, hierarchical structures they will need to negotiate and sustain when they do finally reach the workplace and full citizenship. Schooling commodifies, fragments and packages learning and education. Specialists are paid to do the work of the community and in return the community gets diplomas and degrees for their children. The rich white male vanguard of the consolidated culture invented and eventually imposed schooling throughout its global reach. Visit a small, rural schoolhouse in Kenya where there is no white man in sight, but then imagine the schoolhouse strung up like a marionette puppet with elite white guys pulling the strings. All schools are white schools in this fundamental sense. All are male schools in the same way and all ultimately serve the systems of the consolidated culture that benefit the ruling, affluent classes very disproportionately. The same is true, generally, of all the institutions we live by and through. If there is a learning organization that is neither hierarchical nor commodified and its curricular content does not condition students to play the games of the consolidated culture, then such a place should probably be called something other than a 'school'.

Though our lives today continue to become more dependent on hierarchical institutions and commodified products (including service products), remnants of the tribal model continue to operate between the cracks. Though, for example, the programmatic substance of Alcoholics Anonymous does not in any way look beyond the consolidated culture, this association is neither hierarchical nor commodified in structure. AA meets needs through the power of people coming together, facing each other and sharing and exchanging their unique gifts, personal experience and caring support. All are essentially equal in status and respected as teachers. Informal, mutual exchange networks still operate within families and, particularly in poorer and immigrant communities, within extended families and villages.

'Institutional racism' is a concept introduced a few decades back to address a dimension of racism that is deeper, more pervasive and therefore more oppressive than the personal dimension of overt, personal bigotry and discrimination. But looking at the genesis and evolution of our culture as a whole, it appears to me that a deeper, more pervasive and long-standing dimension of racism (and classism and sexism) than what we've come to refer to as 'institutional racism' is the racism inherent in the institutional structure itself. It's not simply that what goes on within some institutions is institutionally racist, but that racism is inherent in the structural form of the institution itself. A tragic consequence of not seeing this dimension of racism is that freedom struggles are largely confined to equalizing opportunities and rewards within the basic hierarchical, competitive, commodified structures of our institutions. If the consolidated culture game is baseball, our justice struggles amount to securing more at bats and more batting practice — perhaps equal access to the dugout — for traditionally marginalized Hacky Sack players. Racism's fundamental tension line is not between races within our culture and its systems/structures but between our consolidated global monoculture and the very different way of thinking and living represented by cultures (and their members of color) living outside or on the edges of our imperial strongholds. Forms of racism within our culture are derivative of this fundamental tension line, though the suffering and oppression may not be any less severe.

It's not as if powerful, affluent white men rule the world they've seized through their structures and institutions, but more that our world is ruled by the steamroller culture itself, created and passed on initially by affluent, powerful white men to maximize benefits to this category of people. At a certain point, the culture evolves on its own and drives and shapes how we think and live as if it had a mind and will of its own, a will determined to make whatever adjustments are necessary — turn the screws more or yield a little — to sustain and extend itself. The essential lesson is that only a fundamental shift away from the consolidated culture and toward some form or forms of community-based alternatives will lead to equality and dignity for all people. This requires a shift that is fundamentally cultural, not political (in the usual sense) or economic. Although the gains of the civil rights movement here liberated oppressed blacks to a significant degree within the structural context of the culture, expanding political and economic opportunities within this inherently oppressive social context cannot be the prize at the end of the struggle. Likewise, while European rulers were recently forced out of political leadership and colonial control in the African nations they fabricated, the European legacy dictating how things are run in these countries and how people live together remains essentially in place. A cultural shift that will give birth to new forms of social organization that are not inherently oppressive consists of a change in the way people in our global society collectively think about who we are, where we came from and where we are heading. We have to let go of the consolidated culture and its mythology.

Individuals have been experiencing this shift in perspective gradually over centuries and, it seems to me, more quickly in recent decades. Change comes from individuals thinking differently, teaching others and experimenting with alternatives to the dominant models. Yet one of the most obstructive beliefs we hold collectively at the core of our cultural mythology is individualism and the illusion of separateness. To locate the source of both our oppression and our liberation in our culture instead of in individual people and institutions is perhaps the first and most critical step in breaking through. There are very bigoted individuals and cruelly oppressive, violent institutions, but they aren't the primary enemy. Our culture is itself a system and it is the system that shapes and drives most of what we all do on a daily basis. We can overlook — and even mask and therefore reinforce in some respects — this deeply cultural basis of racism when we direct our resistance to personal expressions of bigotry, as necessary as this always is in some form. Attention to personal acts and expressions of racism, especially when spread in the mainstream media, can leave whites who are less overtly racist somewhat complacent and righteous. In the moral, spiritual, social, political and cultural chaos of our 21st century world, there are thousands of cross currents challenging the dominant culture from all sides and angles.

The consolidated culture has prevailed over tribal cultures as well as other civilizations by the force of its violence, missionary zeal and need to constantly grow and expand. It got its start in the Fertile Crescent region of the Near East. Agricultural Revolutions similar to ours occurred independently in several locations around the globe, but the unique combination of cultural mythology and practices that evolved from our Fertile Crescent experiments disposed and enabled us to conquer the world and assimilate other tribal and civilizational cultures. The conquest is still in progress, but over the past few centuries much assimilation and consolidation has been achieved. During this period, the African continent was conquered and stamped in the image of the consolidated culture (there are a few tribes holding ground). The Americas were taken over (only a few tribes left to bring in), and the Asian continent, with its distinct and highly developed Chinese and Indian civilizations, and also including many tribal societies, is still blending into our way of life.

*****

I lived through all the millennia of this cultural experiment and despite its promising start, I believe we should cut our heavy losses and abandon it. Though it gives the world many beautiful things every day, our culture is also a cancer taking over the body, the body of human life on the planet. In spite of protections and opportunities provided by the human rights movements, our culture's systems continue to crush much of the human population and lock even the privileged now into a way of life that is increasingly isolated, sterile, hurried and artificial. Not to mention that our wasteful consumerism is causing our growing population to destroy its own habitat (the planet at this point). We're sucking the earth up into our bodies and amenities at a rate that will, unchecked, extinguish us all in just a very short time. The money system we've developed to help us suck has most recently slammed into its growth limit wall. Not a good indicator of longevity.

And I've lived through the generations as a privileged class individual for the most part. Never a top guy, I've nevertheless always had it relatively easy. My skin color, my gender, my sexual orientation, my class position all opened the silo doors without much effort. Someone said of the first George Bush that he was born on third base (sticking with the baseball metaphor) but insisted he hit a triple. That's a blinding privilege. Many times, consistently at least through the last couple millennia, I have spoken out and acted on behalf of justice and expanded opportunities for marginalized people. But with the passing of each century I always looked back on the century before in amazement of how cruel we were to each other, prompting me (and many others) to ask, "How could we/they have done that?" And since I was there at the time, I had to ask myself, "How could *I* have done that?" I consequently call myself the guiltiest man alive because I acquiesced in and benefited from a variety of cruelly oppressive systems, including, for example, various forms of slavery. The thing of it is, I've observed, is that every 'we' of the current generation becomes a 'they' when the generation passes. I have solid inductive reason to assume that the generations alive today, now pointing fingers at the barbarity of slavery, gender oppression and colonialism of days gone by, will be subject to the similar judgment of the next. Particularly if we manage to chart a new cultural path in the coming few years, I can well imagine our great grandchildren scratching their heads mightily trying to fathom how we could've done some of the things we are now doing without a flinch. Our descendants may point the finger at you and at me, call us immoral or deficient, or they may simply be grateful that their world has rid itself of the omnicidal culture. Like a demon we all collectively hold together (culture isn't an individual matter), we need to undertake a cultural self-exorcism.

Every moment of the day I can choose to accept or to renounce privilege. On this level I am guilty as accused when I choose privilege. But there's a level on which all people in all cultures are compelled to do what people around them are doing, usually because it's the path of least resistance to survival and perceived happiness for self and family. That's me, too. We can choose to try to make people better than they are and thereby flail hopelessly at the force of the dominant culture, or we can be agents of cultural transformation. A culture that is functional, sustainable and freedom-giving will make it relatively easy for people with the usual virtues and vices to survive and live well, connected in meaningful ways to each other and to the earth. That's the way I want to go out.

What Does it Mean to
Give Up on Our World?

A very dear mentor recently declared, in other words, that she had given up. Giving up has long been a live option for most social activists. How many of us can admit to not ever noticing it? I can think of three reasons why it is useful to tease out the subtleties of actually pressing the 'give up' lever:

1. "I give up," in the context of a longish activist run, is easily received as a categorical declaration, meaning little without qualification;

2. So, to give up Y sometimes means to free time and energy up to focus instead on X, not simply to either fully escape the world or commit suicide, or even to abandon activism;

3. Giving up, at least in the activist world, has a disturbing and negative reputation that is somewhere between underserved and highly exaggerated.

Few would contest the decision to give up the activist life to preserve personal health or sanity. Sad, but understandable. Neglecting basic self-care is a reliable cause of burnout. Below the surface, however, often lies an expectation that reliably goes unmet. This disappointment is the quiet killer, constantly nurturing the more superficial symptoms of the activists' passionate, fast-paced lifestyle. The expectation, simple and reasonable, is that social action will 'change the world' and/or 'make a difference'. Indeed, with a persistent application of organized pressure, our systems, structures and institutions can become marginally kinder and gentler. This is the activist's victory, worthy of celebration, but also painfully limited. Institutions are generally more responsive to change pressure than are social structures such as laws and legal frameworks, which are more vulnerable than are the systems, such as the economy, that support these structures. Large institutions are generally harder than small ones, and so on. The intransigence of all three (institutions, structures and systems) is reinforced by the necessary way in which they must, in a self-organized manner, nest within each other's parameters — institutions roughly nest within their wider structures, which nest within supporting systems. Large social systems must nest within the parameters of culture and its narrative. All totaled up, therefore, this thing we wish to change seems like an unmovable edifice. It normally is.

Removing all advantages wealthy Americans currently enjoy in the influence of elections would create a significant change in the political system here in the U.S. from the perspective of those far-sighted activists plugging away in this direction. Victory here is highly unlikely, but conceivable. It is likewise conceivable that our world will achieve the U.N. Millennial Goal of ensuring an adequate supply of safe drinking water to all of its people (especially since our world spends three times more on bottled water in a year — over one hundred billion — than it would take to achieve this goal. Easy!). Not so sure about reversing runaway climate change. Indeed, war, poverty and power imbalances can be virtually eliminated, at least for a time, with a few key switch flips, redirecting the currents, shutting some off, turning others on. The quiet killer is the assumption that these unimaginable victories, easy to achieve if the necessary number of people in high enough places wake up one day suddenly inspired to flip these switches, are *practically* achievable, not just theoretically achievable, and without abandoning the edifice of nested institutions, structures, systems and culture. Ninety-nine percent of change efforts, including self-labeled 'radical' ones, are not headed in the direction of moving the edifice, only softening it. The election and subsequent presidency of Barack Obama reflect this promise/disappointment cycle for many.

"People know what they do," observed philosopher Michael Foucault, and "frequently they know why they do what they do; but what they don't know is what what they do does." We know we are trying to achieve justice, but we are not aware of just how little our finest victories budge the edifice of injustice. On a level, the victories even undergird the edifice by making life within its pyramidal stone walls more endurable. I believe that the frustration of this Sisyphean predicament is *felt* long before it is fully *seen* for what it is. Hence, burnout, resignation, and giving up.

When 'giving up' means abandoning hope and faith in the responsiveness of the edifice, giving up can and should, I think, be liberating rather than debilitating. My beloved mentor went down because while she embraced and articulated a vision that extended to a reshaped world far beyond the nested systems of our world order, she could not or would not look beyond its confines for a vehicle to *get* us to this vision. Or, at the very least, she invested in alternative cultural stories and systems but could still not relinquish the assumption that the edifice must in some specific and recognizable form come with her and us to the promised land, as collaborating partners. Some elements of the edifice surely *will* survive this transition, but we defeat ourselves if we are *dependent* on any partnership like this, especially at the national level.

After twenty years of pyramid-softening political activism, I gave up myself. Maybe ten percent of my effort continues to push the government or a big corporation to change something (typically, to *stop* doing something), but my apparent withdrawal from the activist community — after a period of learning and soul-searching — really amounted to a shift in thinking and energy investment. Most of my effort has, in the *past* twenty years, been directed to persuading others to 'give up' on the pyramid and begin tinkering with alternative systems, structures and institutions. I realized that our culture and the systems, structures and institutions that have evolved with it are going to compel us to compete with each other, using the available (i.e., culturally supported) tools, and reward both the winners and their heirs with a bounty of wealth, power and status. The zero-sum competition translates into this bounty being mercilessly sucked from the people lower on the pyramid and from the earth. Though conceivable, it is practically impossible to make this arrangement serve a very different purpose. "Systems create their own behavior," according to systems activist Donella Meadows, another mentor. Individual people, each one theoretically vulnerable to dramatic personal conversion, are nonetheless and otherwise *not* the source of power in our world — systems are, including the culture — itself a system — that creates and sustains them.

It's a wicked knot the caring activist — and also nurse and schoolteacher and other caring servicers — are caught in, yet no one's to blame for this tragedy. Our global economic system, and all of our social subsystems, behave predictably. As the Zen master waits for the novice to 'give up' on thinking through the puzzles of life, our next world is waiting for us to 'give up' on this one. To stop pounding the pyramid and climb down and off, to walk away.

But what is 'world'? "I give up on the 'world'," and "We can't save the 'world'," or, my mother's fave, "The 'world's' going to hell in a hand basket (?)," are among the frequently declared generalizations begging at least one question: what is the/our 'world'? If 'world' refers to everything human (of which we are collectively aware), giving *that* up is serious, deep and disturbing. There are considerations that make giving up on *this* 'world' understandable, to me, and on some days, justified. Humans are killing the planet.

The 'world' and the 'planet' are often, mostly unconsciously, conflated: 'World' = 'Planet'. The reason we slip into this conflation is that our 'world', once limited to a very small geographical portion of the planet, has gone global and now covers the whole entire sphere. Though the 'world' as planet appears to be dying, there's no giving up here, at least among those of us not anticipating a heavenly world.

But just as our 'world' history books distinguish in the middle chapters between the 'New World' and 'Old World', the definition I find appropriate for most contexts is "the sphere — and systems — of known human activity within the (vague) boundaries of (our) civilization." When these boundaries did not extend across the Atlantic before 1492 the 'world' didn't either. The 'New World' was inhabited by people living tribally and generally without the pyramidal systems, structures and institutions of the 'Old World'. Tribal societies living today in pockets protected from civilizational encroachment live in worlds that are likewise not ours, though their existence and whereabouts, perhaps something of their activity, may be known by some of us. Globalization can be understood as the unifying absorption of 'worlds', in this sense. Our globalizing world now includes and controls all but a tiny fraction of the planet's entire human population, the outliers being the same isolated tribes. References to 'Eastern Civilization' as distinct from 'Western Civilization' (as in, 'East is East, West is West...') have receded. The ancient civilizations of China and India have merged with each other and with the Big West. Little need to call what we have now anything but 'Civilization', which, by this definition of the 'world', is essentially the same *thing* as the 'world'.

Ironically, giving up on *this* 'world' might in fact be a necessary step to saving humanity as a whole, as a species that is, as well as many other species. The culture, systems, structures and institutions that define our world have proven incapable of meeting human needs adequately and interfacing sustainably with the planet's systems. Abandoning and walking away is the appropriate measure to take. My personal challenge, as a 'walk away' activist, as a defector rather than a reformer or revolutionary, is to discern which strategies actually point in this direction. Each proposal is subject to debate. Many initiatives necessarily rely on the institutions, structures and systems of our world, yet still point and push beyond them. Hard to know. Within institutions of 'higher' learning, I have been teaching courses that have exposed thousands of college students to this conversation — "What must we do, what do we need, to get the world we want?" And after class I still go to the grocer to buy food with the money I make from doing this. Likewise, somebody paid something for people to read my essays about this. But many of those college students are, at various levels, ready to walk away. Some may already have, in some manner, in some sense. They may not *look* like they're ready, finishing their degree, working their jobs, but they've been exposed to the conversation, probably others like it, and are peeking out and around. I think of my teaching work, together with many workshops I've facilitated, as cultural activism, looking to change how we think about ourselves and our world, and about change itself.

Defection activism can certainly consist of living outside the food, shelter and power grids, particularly if a *group* of people tries this. But I also believe that the community-building work I have been doing in my city neighborhoods over the past twenty years, though not so dramatic, leans in the direction of walking away. Helping neighbors turn to one another, as equals, to extend and receive support, reacquaints us with our tribal roots and delinks us a bit from the dollar economy. It's practice, I suppose. Alcoholics Anonymous does something like this too. What is 'radical'?

There are lots of experiments activists are undertaking that inspire me, that seem to show the way out, to open the door. Not to get stuck on judging individual trials, we must focus first on our activist orientation and ask our own selves, "Am I devoting my activist energy to systemic reform and maintenance, or am I doing something to help move us out and away?" We are powerless to get our world's entrenched systems to behave differently than they have, do and will, much like the recovering alcoholic is powerless to make his life do what he wants for him while drinking every waking hour. Let us give up and get going.

How I Backed into Loving the World

Until now I haven't felt like telling anyone I loved everybody. I didn't really think much of it — it was, after all and more precisely, a *recognition* of a change that had already occurred, and very *gradually* at that, not itself a change. And what kind of world lover is a braggart? I'm coming out here because my experience learning to love may in some way help others love, and love is good. Additionally, while I genuinely value my years trying to be a saintly lover, and how far and in what ways I measured up, I'm neither as good nor ambitious as I once was and I feel both content with the 'demotion' and also a little relieved. On the one hand, the love continued to deepen and expand, on the other, I feel like I can appreciate this development without associating it with holiness or supernatural virtue. It's just there. Good. And so, by the way, is watching a football game every autumn weekend with friends and beer. Not as good, certainly, but there. Loving all the humans is something I imagine lots of people do. Many are born that way it seems.

One day last year, I emerged from morning meditation and discovered that I loved each and every human I knew and knew of, and, by a crude extrapolation, all the rest. (I'm lucky one of them isn't beating or belittling me on a regular basis, for sure. Privilege and good fortune helped make this happen, in my case.) It was a pleasant enough realization, but not one that conferred more than a whiff of feeling special. Yes, I love the hated Koch Brothers, the hated Barack Obama, the hated Rush Limbaugh, the hated Jon Stewart (Are there actual people who *hate* Jon Stewart?). Strange to feel, a lapsed monk, the sensation of loving the world, and the humans who created and recreate it.

Some days I'm tempted to detest us all. The survival chances and prosperity of virtually every other life species sharing the planet would improve without us on it. I was impressed by the way one of my incarcerated students laid it out: "It stands to reason we treat the land like shit because we treat each *other* like shit." No contest. The horribleness of our horrible behavior cannot be denied or exaggerated.

Still, I love the humans, all of them. I decided it was worth a try, for the sake of sharing, to account for this unlikely yet welcome development in my life. What I discovered surprised me.

*****

Of the several conditions working in my mind-body urging a loving orientation toward all humans, the psychologist would surely underscore my good fortune to have been loved by many humans since babyhood. I did feel loved, cared for and consistently *valued* as a kid growing up in New Jersey, America. A reinforcing feedback loop kept me on the love track: I loved others because I was loved and I loved even more to sustain and expand being loved. Many people are lucky this way, to get trapped in a virtuous cycle of love. Others come to kindness in other ways. The shadow side of this cycle, in the service of full disclosure, is a dependence on love and approval that is not always personally or socially beneficial. The virtuous cycle can also be an unhealthy dependency cycle. Never sure where I was or am.

In my twenties and thirties (I'm around sixty now), my personal mission was to renounce privilege. Not, certainly not, the privilege of growing up loved, but the privilege of also growing up in suburban middle class whiteness.[*] Fancy college education, all expenses paid by devoted, professional parents. They put five kids through. Then in my college years I got mugged by Jesus, Francis, Gandhi, Dorothy, Thoreau. Practicing nonviolence and simplicity as a lifestyle, I learned to love the homeless and hungry men I later served at Amos House, the Providence Catholic Worker-style shelter and soup kitchen I lived and worked in for many years. My brothers, all of them. Some I didn't like very much. Loving doesn't mean liking, but soon after realizing and appreciating my love for people, I experienced the corollary sensation that I didn't seem to dislike as many people, and/or dislike them as

---

[*] 'Whiteness' and 'White' are placed in quotes to distinguish this label from a strictly racial pointer. Light skin pigment is a quick identifying marker signaling a culturally supported status rank that is higher than people of color, but 'white' more broadly refers to a *cultural* pointer that privileges those in our global society who occupy higher status rungs by virtue of being or becoming successful by culturally sanctioned means.

intensely, as most people around me seemed to. A residual effect, I suppose.

What does it mean to love, if disliking is compatible with loving? About love plenty has been written. I associate 'love' with 'care'; to love another is to be disposed — ready — to actively care for her. However, this is really an inner circle association for me. I'm not disposed to actively care for Dick Cheney, unless I stumbled upon him fallen to the gutter (a literal gutter). Agape, as some in the Jesus tradition call the kind of love for all humans I mean here, is more about understanding, appreciating and celebrating the beautiful humanness — and divinity — of every person. 'God in all', as the Quakers teach. I don't like Donald Trump so much and will not care for him, but I can see into his essential humanity, his basic human aspirations. He wants to be loved, he shares my needs.

The spirit, principles and strategies of nonviolence trained me to love the political and corporate leaders my peace and justice groups campaigned against. I cultivated relationships with them by mixing love with a resolute unwillingness to be intimidated. I've always addressed people, regardless of place and position, by first name. Quakers, again, taught me this — to renounce titles. It reflects a mix of love and dignity. I love you, but as my equal, though you may appear at the moment in front of me as an 'enemy', or a 'superior'. The mix disarms and clears the way for human-to-human connection. It often works. Otherwise, it's just a way of being in the world. I've developed short and longer-term relationships with 'enemy' police and security officers on these terms. Another virtuous cycle augmenting the childhood loop. The more I love —

instead of fear — those on the other side, and the more this serves to connect rather than alienate, the more I want to sustain this interpersonal flow.

I can't tell if the daily yoga and running rituals I established coming out of college added anything to the love, but any ritual that improves bodily health, equanimity and mindfulness must encourage loving.

Still in my twenties, I took the *Course in Miracles*, while working at the soup kitchen. The Course instructions claimed that over time, praying and reflecting on its daily lessons will transform the student's orientation to the world, and to the humans in particular. Residual lessons from the course still surface in my daily prayer thirty-four years later. "Forgiveness brings to the world all of its joy." Could be something to the transformational claim. I never *noticed* an improvement, can't be sure of a causal connection, but I repeat this lesson every morning and I *have* come to love more.

In addition to helping me recognize and appreciate the love in my heart, meditation also probably nurtured this love. I sit for about a half hour on the city park lake bank before and after a short meditative walk, which includes prayer and a little chanting. That short time permits at least *some* connection — to the earth and sky there, and the wider world and planet — and some personal disarmament, a brief moment of unself-consciousness, a shedding of ego bits. Love is connection consciousness, not as a final achievement, but at the very heart and beginning of love.

Finally, and the central finding I wish to share, the factors that pried me over the top in love were not psycho-spiritual, but more cognitive in nature. I learned in a deep and abiding way, that humans, and the way humans think and behave, are not the same as the people of our globalized monoculture. While learning this, I also learned about the power and dynamics of *systems*. I acquired from these lessons a profound forgiveness that added a new and surprising dimension to my love for the people. Learning to vaguely see and partially understand systems opened my heart, particularly as I began to see and understand *culture* as a system.

This takes some explaining.

Individuals share very similar basic needs and they normally apply themselves to meeting them, but they do this in wildly different ways, depending on the cultural context — their culture(s) and their unique response to their culture(s). Food, clothing, shelter and health insurance are technically not basic human needs, but *satisfiers* of our basic needs for health and protection.[*] I count love and belonging as basic human needs, but shopping and pornography as unconsciously perceived satisfiers of this need. The observed virtue of Amish people and nobility of untainted tribal people are as deceptive as the perceived crassness of court TV addicts and greediness of hedge fund traders. Same needs, same self-interest, very different satisfiers, very different satisfier options.

---

[*] See Manfred A. Max-Neef, *Human Scale Development Conception Application and Further Reflection*, Apex Press (1989), chapter 2.

Creating and presenting the satisfier menu is, within environmental constraints, the job of culture. Culture is an assortment of collectively held beliefs and applied behaviors, somewhat like the body is an assortment of parts and behaviors that work with and reinforce each other to optimize health. We live in a time of unusual cultural chaos and change, but comparatively intact and isolated cultures resemble much more closely the body system model — parts working together, making a coherent whole, aiming at survival and optimal prosperity. Bodies change, they evolve, cultures change, they evolve. Slowly, as a rule; rapidly, as the exception. Our globalized monoculture is changing rapidly, due to the forces of globalization (= cultural integration and assimilation) and widespread disaffection, contention and resistance.

A system is an assortment of parts making a whole by working together to achieve a unified purpose. Conscious intention as we typically associate with 'purpose' is not a requirement. Like all cultures, ours is a collection of parts struggling to work together to achieve a purpose, as if this all has a will and mind of its own. Yet, though there is no conscious intention, or intelligent design and execution, the cultural system is a unifying force pushing and shaping what we think and do. To forgive and love the human individuals, I have found it very helpful to view culture this way, to see and understand the humans in their cultural context.

The 'parts' of culture, ours and all others, are sometimes called 'memes'* — cultural bits of all sizes and shapes, ideas and behaviors. Just as physical life emerged and evolved on our planet through the self-organizing of particle-waves, mutations and adjustments, so have human cultures emerged and evolved through the self-organized interaction of memes, people's ideas and behaviors. The gradualism of cultural evolution makes it hazardous to pinpoint a culture's birthdate and place. I think ancient Mesopotamia, however, the starting time and place of our classic world history texts, is serviceable as a birthdate and place for our culture, now global in reach.

The culture of western civilization emerged in response to changing material conditions in the Fertile Crescent region. Success in growing large quantities of grain led to an exponential population explosion that continues today.† Over millennia, the cultural response to this expansion laid the memetic cornerstones of our modern global culture. Along with spectacular technological innovation, art, science and philosophy, our culture developed a messianic compulsion to convert and absorb tribal groups living on the edge of its ever-expanding frontier as more land and resources were

---

* See Richard Dawkins, *The Selfish Gene*, Oxford (1989), chapter 11.

† Exponential growth refers to a growth pattern, as in a bank account balance increasing on a *compounding* interest rate, through which numbers increase by a near constant percentage. As in a bank account, capital gains might appear modest for a long period but eventually yield balance doublings over short periods, or, slow growth at first, then all of a sudden. See Albert A. Bartlett's explanation:
http://youtube.com/watch?v=u5iFESMAU58

needed to feed expansion. Torn from their tribal communities, many victims were killed or displaced rather than assimilated. The economic meme of expansion (the civilization and its economy must grow, or die) is mutually reinforced by the meme of hierarchy: humans are separate from, superior to and lords over other life forms, which exist to serve us; civilized people trump indigenous people in a similar way, and wealthy, powerful, 'white' people within our culture stand over the rest, who are subservient and inferior.

These and other cornerstone memes of our culture generate subsystems, such as the economic and political systems that have succeeded each other over time, and also the kinds of social structures and institutions we have come to live in, by, for and with. At the institutional policy level, leaders consciously make decisions that influence and manage how their followers think and act. But otherwise, our culture — as system — is a product of unconscious self-organization, the evolution of memes contesting with each other for survival in the cultural meme pool. Capitalism's apologists have at times insisted that its favored economic system organically evolved and therefore is as natural and inevitable as it is virtuous, in contrast to the programmatic contrivance that is state socialism.* A 'cultural fallacy' refers to mistaking features of one's culture for features of humanity as a whole, or of 'human nature'. Capitalist and socialist economic structures are equally

---

* See Michael Perelman, *The Invention of Capitalism: Classical Political Economy and the Secret History of Primitive Accumulation*, Duke University Press (2000).

products of deliberate public policy decisions *and* the wider formative basket of civilizational culture. Socialists may insist that theirs is at least a *counter*cultural innovation, but neither system describes how humans are *meant* to arrange their economic lives or how humans have naturally evolved.

So while the powerful make decisions that profoundly affect the lives of everyone else, these same decision-makers and their decisions are themselves dictated by cultural memes and systems beyond their control and even beyond their awareness. Our culture's notion of 'free will' provides a practical decision-making framework at the personal and social levels, but on a deeper level, this meme is a delusion. As the culture presses for expansion, it also fragments — communities into nuclear families and families into isolated individuals. Creating the illusion of metaphysical freedom (as in 'free will') reinforces our culture's rugged individualism while the culture itself, its systems and structures, shape and drive personal thought and behavior.

Individuals certainly do buck the cultural flow, especially in today's world rich with a variety of countercultural crosscurrents. But while you never see a grown adult walking naked down a city street in the broad daylight of a summer's day, harming no one, you can witness each day hundreds of workers filing into my state's nuclear submarine factory to build huge seafaring weapons of mass destruction. Innocuous public nudity is not culturally supported (we're not 'animals' after all!), prepping to incinerate the world apparently is.

ystems rule. Culture, as a system, and culture's hierarchy of subsystems, shape and drive, constrain and encourage how we think and behave, down to small details. Our dominant culture and global, money economy selects for material ambition and acquisitiveness. It predictably produces greed, corruption and hyper-consumerism. While our cultural systems fragment our lives in so many ways, they also evolved to support mass society. In this sense, the culture of civilization constitutes a mutation, or experimental departure from small-scale, egalitarian tribal communities. Research suggests that humans cannot maintain affinity — working relationships — with more than one hundred and fifty individuals.[*] The tribal form of social organization, tested out for hundreds of thousands of years, accommodates this limitation. We have applied many systemic techniques to make human life work in mass society that attempt to *override* it. Traffic lights, legal contracts, institutions as we know them. Growing up in a mass society of strangers, people will think, feel and behave very differently than they will growing up in a small community.

In the 1950's, researchers conducted an experiment in which mice were put in a cage that included food and water receptacles and also a lever, which, when pushed by the mouse, directed electrical currents to stimulate pleasure centers in its brain. Pushing the lever made him feel good. In short order, the mouse became too preoccupied with lever pushing to take enough time to eat. A classic case of addiction formation, but

[*] See Robin Dunbar, *How Many Friends Does One Person Need? Dunbar's Number and Other Evolutionary Quirks.* London: Faber & Faber (2010).

also a useful metaphor for systems thinking. We shouldn't conclude that there's something wrong with the mouse (the experimenter, yes, but not the mouse), some innate flaw or natural desire to pleasure himself to death. Animals *are* born able to experience pleasure — that's the extent of it. One simple way to explain the steroidal greed and acquisitiveness we frequently blame for economic downturns and species extinction is that behavior causing outcomes like these are predictable inside the cage of the social systems we have created and sustain. We keep hating on each other in the cage, but we can't see the cage and that our 'home' is somewhere quite outside, beyond the invisible bars. Systems thinking helps us see the bars and the cage and then to also lighten up and back off each other.

Garrett Hardin concludes from his "Tragedy of the Commons" exposition that "the morality of an act cannot be determined from a photograph...but is a function of the state of the system at the time it is performed."[*] Systems theorist Donella Meadows identifies a series of systems 'traps', like the commons tragedy in which the fully rational and understandable judgment of herders separated from each other by a vast unowned commons will nevertheless lead to the valuable commons' destruction and the demise of all herding as grazing sheep gradually multiply and graze out the common pasture. Many interrelated dimensions of our global world are currently trapped in an exponential growth pattern that is leading to what should feel like an abrupt crash in the systems that

---

[*] Garrett Hardin, "The Tragedy of the Commons," *Science*, Dec. 13, 1968.

support us. This trap is centuries in the making, but is pinching us more deeply in recent decades. That is the character of exponential growth. Simply by going about the daily business of our normal living, we make our own deathbed by contributing to collective systemic tragedies like these. Our morality, rationality and self-interest are 'bounded' by the systems we move in and through. So instead of blaming and correcting individuals and institutions and fretting over predictable events, Meadows offers this version of the splendid 'serenity prayer': "God grant us the serenity to exercise our bounded rationality freely in the systems that are structured appropriately, the courage to restructure the systems that aren't, and the wisdom to know the difference."[*]

This perspective offers another way of challenging the mythology of 'innate depravity' and 'original sin'. We aren't born ignorant (in need of enlightenment) or morally corrupt (in need of redemption). We're born into the cage of a social system that has proven incapable of meeting basic human needs and caused a host of trouble on the planet. Our cage is also collapsing on us, to extend the metaphor. We experience this collapse on many levels and fronts, including a widening generation gap and ecological overshoot. Fortunately, young people worldwide are increasingly resistant to internalizing the cultural and systemic program of their parents. It is time to love one another and also to get out. The call to love is also, in this urgent sense, a call to defect.

---

[*] Donella Meadows, *Thinking in Systems, a primer*, 110, Chelsea Green (2008).

Gratitude

If this collection of essays could feel and express gratitude, it should thank for the evolution of its thought stream: Daniel Quinn and his Austin Seminar (1997), Joanna Macy and her 'Work that Reconnects' workshop, Keith Morton and tom king. For their contribution to this evolution and also for their support and encouragement in writing, thanks to Philip Edmonds, Nisha Purushotham, Rick Benjamin and our 'Reimagining Social Change' conversation partners, Karina Lutz and C.S. Drury (also the book's publisher).

ABOUT THE AUTHOR

Jim facilitates workshops on community building, cultural transformation, systems thinking and also, with Karina Lutz, 'Work that Reconnects' (deep ecology) retreats. He teaches Philosophy, Community Service and Global Studies at the Community College of Rhode Island, Providence College and Rhode Island's state prison. In the summer of 2015, Jim and a small group of friends founded Listening Tree Cooperative, a community-based permaculture homestead, in Chepachet, Rhode Island (www.listeningtree.coop). For much of his work life, Jim served as the co-director of Amos House, a homeless shelter and soup kitchen on Providence's south side, while organizing dozens of campaigns promoting peace and justice. He is father to Sofia (b. 1991) and Nelson (1994).